PRAISE FOR
LIVING WITH BIPOLAR

"In this book Xavier bears witness to trauma and distress but also awareness and recovery in a way that positions narrative above pathology and reflection above trauma. Lived experience stories are more important than ever in a period where we are on the cusp of fundamental changes in psychiatry. We can no longer tolerate a mental health system that does not include the humanities and Michael's evocative art drives home the imperative for creative depictions of mental health, but more; creative lives defined by self expression and self-determination."

- Professor Paul Rhodes, School of Psychology, University of Sydney

"It dawned on me, as I read Xavier's story, that even though mental illness is so common, few people get to tell their story, and even fewer have them published. Xavier's account highlights the isolation that comes with mental illness. Sharing these stories is an important way to reduce that isolation and lessen the stigma for people with mental illness. Xavier's book carries a powerful message: you're not alone, others have faced similar struggles and learned to manage them. It's valuable for young people to read how Xavier has managed his moods, offering inspiration to those early in their journey with mental illness. His story is one of resilience, growth, and, most importantly, hope."

- Dr Rachael Murrihy, Kidman Centre, UTS

Living With Bipolar

For years you search, berate and hope.
You wander wounded.
Then the answer arrives and it's not a resolution.
It's the beginning of understanding.

Written by Xavier Coy
Illustrated by Michael Arvithis

Published in 2024 by ORiGiN Imprint,
an imprint of the ORiGiN™ Music Group.

ORiGiN™ Imprint
Ground Floor, 47-49 Murray Street
Pyrmont NSW 2009

www.originimprint.com

All rights reserved. No part of this publication may be reproduced, stored in a retrieval system or transmitted in any form by any means, electronic, mechanical, photocopying, recording or otherwise, without the prior written permission of the publishers and copyright holders.

The moral rights of the author have been asserted.

Copyright text and concept © Xavier Coy & Michael Arvithis 2024
Copyright illustrations © Michael Arvithis 2024
Typesetting by Amber Quin

Printed in Australia by Lightning Source

Dedicated to

Vasilios Arvithis

Contents

Preface	1
Introduction	7
Depressive State	8
Melancholia	11
Not Enjoying Things You Used To	12
Inability To Accept Love	15
Lack of Self Worth	17
Fatigue	18
Uncontrollable Crying	21
Appetite	22
Hopelessness	25
Misery & Despair	26
The Middle Ground	28
Sleep	28
Memory Loss	33
Avoiding Eye Contact	34
Anger	37
Unwanted Thoughts	38
Shamefulness & Regret	41
Lack of Control	42
Hypomanic State	45
Anxiety	46
Agitation	49
Restlessness	50
Inability to Sit Still or Focus	53
Frenzied Speaking	54
Risk Taking Behaviour	57
Grandeur	58
Euphoria	61
Energy	62

Disorganised Behaviour	65
The Elephant In The Room...	66
A New Life	68
Diagnosis	69
Medication	70
Speak Up & Ask For Help	71
Therapy	72
Booze & Drugs Aren't The Answer	73
Let Go Of The Past & Forgive Yourself	74
Learn To Love Yourself	75
Philosophy	76
Art	77
Writing & Creativity	78
Nature	79
Explore	80
Exercise	81
Moderate	82
Practice Gratitude	83
Stay True To Yourself	84
Value Your Friends & Family & Choose Them Wisely	85
Epilogue	86
Acknowledgements	**88**
About	**89**

Preface

At the age of twenty-eight I was diagnosed with bipolar disorder. By the time I was diagnosed I'd experienced many years of struggling with my mental health. The only surprise in getting diagnosed with bipolar was how long it took to get there. The trail of breadcrumbs left behind looked mountainous to me. Over the years I have tried to pin point moments that could have contributed to me having bipolar. The reality is that there are many I could pick. I can look back and see times when I was unhappy, times when I was in trouble but not knowing or being able to understand what was happening.

My roots are in playwriting and screenwriting. The first thing I wrote was a play. It was semi-autobiographical and my first attempt to truly figure out why I am the way I am.

I started writing as a way to rid myself of pain and I quickly discovered that creating story was my vocation. All these ideas and problems that were weighing me down could be explored in story. That's when things started making sense for me. Story was cause and effect. So, life must be too. We are all a culmination of our experiences. We are equipped with tools to make decisions based on those experiences.

****

My parent's split when I was eighteen months old and my sister was six weeks. I can't point to this as anything that would cause any sort of emotional trauma. It didn't. All we knew from when we began walking and talking was that our parents weren't together and that Christmas Eve was with one side of the family and Christmas Day the other. It turns out that the fact they weren't together was far better for us.

We are blessed have the mother we do. Mum was our primary caretaker and relished being a mother. She's always been full of love and warmth. Mum managed to create a home that, despite not having much money, felt like a home where we didn't want for anything. We were encouraged and supported. Since entering my thirties and seeing my friends starting to have children of their own, I marvel more and more at Mum. How she worked full time and raised two children by herself is beyond me.

It's been some years now since I've spoken to my father. He was an inconsistent and often unpleasant part of our childhood. I don't have many memories of him as a little child or in primary school. When looking back with my sister on what it was like being around him comes with a lot of disbelief and confusion. The replica hand gun that shot metal pellets he smuggled through customs to shoot cats in the backyard comes to mind. The perks of being a glorified bus driver in the sky. He was unpredictable and often scary or nasty.

My father was capable of nice things but much more energy was put into the negative. In hindsight he was a bitterly insecure man who needed to assert his aggression and purported superiority and prowess in order to feel good about himself. He desperately needed to be taken seriously and to be seen as important. He was constantly reminding me of how I could never meet his standard. I would be lying if I said this didn't leave a lingering effect on me. In fact, many of the words and actions that were drilled into me as a child are what I'm still unpacking to this day.

My earliest memories of him are these two things. He would say "You'll never be as good as me, you'll never be as smart as me, you'll never be as good looking as me, you'll never be as successful as me." The other was him shadow boxing me saying "There'll be three hits. Me hitting you. You hitting the deck. And the ambulance hitting 100." This turned out to be sadly foreboding minus the ambulance. I have always had issues with my self worth and my inner critic. That voice in your head that tells you that you're not good enough. After years of therapy the etymology is clear. To list all the wild stories would require another book. To avoid any further repercussions, I will keep it to this however it's safe to say what I've included is on the milder side.

Our history and experiences form us. Can this context provide some understanding as to where I am today? I would have to think so.

****

I was recently given hours of footage from my childhood when I was four to five years old. I became obsessed, watching it over and over. As I did, I noticed a pattern in how different how I was depending on the situation. My sister, Matilda, was a wild child. She was pure entertainment and joy, a total extrovert. When at home I was just as wild and confident as my sister, I felt emboldened by her. My Mum, had nothing but loving and sweet words to say. She was kind, positive and patient.

Outside of the house, with other people, it was a different story. I was introverted, painfully shy and unable to talk to strangers. Five year old me was unable to look people I didn't know in the eye. In the footage at home, a place I knew I was safe with Mum, Til, my Nana and Pop, my uncles Pad and James and my aunties Gerri, Jen and Caroline, I was filled with joy. Out in the world I was faced with uncertainty and I didn't have the confidence to deal with it.

There was footage of me at pre-school on an awards day. Every child in the class received an award. My name was last, Xavier usually was, and the teacher missed me. Mum had the camera pointed at me. I had my arms crossed over each other, glued to the chair, it looked like I was creating a shield with my body. One of the other children said "Xavier hasn't got one." The teacher laughed "Oh sorry, Xavier, I forgot you. Xavier's award is for kindness to others and drawing." I practically ran to get the award and tried to run back to my seat to avoid the claps from the parents in attendance.

My Mum called out "Xav" – no luck, I kept my eyes fixed firmly on the floor. "Xavier, come here." There was a melodic delight in her voice. I cuddled her and she whispered "I'm so proud of you." I saw how fearful that little boy was and how much my Mum did to make me feel safe.

Then I came across footage with my father. There were only two short clips out of the hours of footage. Sadly, as predicted, his involvement was negative. The first of the videos was at my fifth birthday party. Mum had organised everything and my father just rocked up. While recording you can hear him mutter "This is the most pathetic party I've ever seen." You could hear her laugh it off, attempting to enjoy the day. I don't know how she didn't tell him to get fucked. Maybe because she knew his rage. It was all negative from him. He criticized, belittled and mocked. I know the behaviour all too well.

The second revealed more about my behaviour around him. It was at my soccer game. The game finishes and he comes up to me and says "Xav, give me a high five." I nervously walk away without acknowledging him. As he follows, I begin to run. He eventually catches up to me as I'm talking to another boy from the team. Then one of the younger brothers, three years old, says to the camera "My brother just won his soccer game." My father mocks back with "And my son won his soccer game too." He calls out to me again and once again and I continue to walk away from him, ignoring him. Eventually I turn around and I say "Where's Mummy?" "She's gone to pick up, Tilly." And that's the end of the exchange. The footage stops shortly after. From the time you learn to crawl you scurry away, when it's time to walk you unlock the door to hide outside and when it's time to run you don't look back and you ask for your Mum.

It was at this time I became obsessed with Batman. The obsession was so deep that all I'd draw at school was Batman, all I'd talk about was Batman and I lived in the Batman costume. The teachers at school met with Mum to discuss the possibility that I was on the Autism spectrum due to the fascination. I wasn't Autistic I was just whole heartedly in love with Batman. When I was pretending to be Batman, I was free, confident and imaginative. It feels like it was an attempt to hide in plain sight. If I could be someone else then I didn't need to be painfully shy anymore.

Embarrassingly, I sucked on a dummy until I was five years old. Some of the home footage showed me walking around with a dummy firmly placed in my mouth. Mum would pick me up from school and I would have a clandestine suck on the dummy in the back seat as Mum would drive away from school. I was latching on to anything that would soothe me. Anything to take away the stress.

In my early primary school years, I started to experience horrific headaches. It got so bad that Mum had to take me to the doctors and they suggested I get an MRI to check if I had a brain tumour.

Before that had to happen, they figured out the problem. I was just incredibly stressed and anxious. I remember falling asleep at night I and fearing that the roof would cave in and crush me while I slept. In the childhood photos of the smiling boy, I can't help but see the boy who was hurting and didn't know why. He had no recourse to fix it. All he knew was his head was hurting and he was scared.

My Dad decided that towards the end of primary school it was appropriate to start giving me beers. My recollection is being about ten years old and having beers at Dad's whenever we visited. As I got older, I saw that drugs and alcohol were a big part of his life which makes the decision to give a child alcohol all the more confusing. I suppose because it was normal to him meant that there was nothing strange about it. I can't imagine that giving a primary school kid booze is the blueprint for a healthy life. Adding alcohol into the brain chemistry of a child must have some sort of impact. To this day I can't understand the thinking behind it and I don't suppose I ever will.

My stress headaches had transferred to ear aches at the end of primary school and into high school. The pain was real however the ear aches only occurred when I was stressed or put in situations where I was overwhelmed. In year six the school had asked me to run for school captain. Afterwards I didn't go to school for three weeks, the whole time the school captain race was on, with an ear ache. Then when high school came around, I had the same problem. I went to the first day and then missed the next two weeks with an ear ache. My first camp in high school I didn't last the night. Mum had to come pick me up because the ear ache struck again. All these occasions came off the back of me being overcome with anxiety. I remember the ear aches but I had to be reminded of the things I missed because of them. I'm sure there were more.

To continue to rattle off all the painful and traumatic moments would require an entire book of its own. There's lots I've left out that happened after this including how violence and gaslighting can cause severe psychological damage. What I've stated before is a taste of what may have been the foundations that pushed me into my teenage years. I started feeling what I thought was just some sadness and worrying a bit. Knowing what I know now it was depression and anxiety. I was struggling. I began seeing a counsellor at high school. Back then I definitely felt the stigma of the kid that had troubles. I didn't want to be seen as a boy who needed therapy. When I was at high school the open dialogue around mental health wasn't there. So, I stopped going and let the cancerous thoughts grow.

In my twenties was when my mental health was really starting to take a stranglehold on me. My mind was dark and chaotic. I'd be manic and bouncing off the walls and then be struck down with the most horrible, pernicious and seemingly inescapable thoughts. I'd feel anger, anxiety, paranoia, deep sorrow, self-loathing and have no idea why. It culminated in an event that changed my life that I'll go into later in the book. It just didn't land until much later than it should have. I saw a psychologist briefly. I was messed up but I wasn't in a place where I really wanted help. I'd go and think I was wasting my time. I'd say all the things I thought they wanted to hear and leave resentful because I'd spent a couple of hundred bucks on some sick game that I won intellectually but bettered me financially. When you're not willing to be helped you can't be.

Eventually it got to a point where I didn't think I would survive if I kept going the way I was. Unless I got help, I was going to spiral further and there was nothing good at the end of that spiral. Life was fear inducing purely because you didn't know whether you were going to be okay when you woke up.

It's not fully known whether bipolar is totally genetic, environmental or socialised. I think in my experience it's all three. After being diagnosed I learnt more of the history of mental health conditions in my family. Of course, as previously mentioned, there are childhood issues that could be pieces, but I simply don't know. It's the not knowing that makes me try and piece the puzzle together. If medical professionals can't give me an answer, then I just have to give myself one. Maybe my bipolar just developed over time. What I believe, however, is that there are clues all along the way of someone who was searching for answers as to why I was in pain. On the first day of COVID lockdown in 2020 was when I was diagnosed. Finally, after all those years, the right outcome was achieved. Living a life with bipolar means there's never a dull moment. As challenging as it is there are upsides and times where you feel like you've been given a gift. Now, as things continue to make sense and aids have been introduced, I can reflect on what this disease is. I'm lucky to have found my answer. Some people don't get that luxury. From here, onwards.

Introduction

BIPOLAR DISORDER IS a wildly misunderstood mental health affliction. Most people's familiarity with bipolar would be depictions in fictional work which often portray the character's as unhinged or so hyperbolic that they become caricature. It pops up in crime documentaries a lot too which is very difficult to watch. On a personal level I've dealt with that misunderstanding first hand. 'Is that the one where you hear voices?' One person asked. Schizophrenia, bipolar, the nutty ones. If you pay attention, you'll hear people jokingly say 'Maybe I/they have bipolar', 'Such a bipolar thing to do', bipolar being the tagline if someone has behaved in an unhinged way or if someone feels a little up and down.

When I didn't understand what was going on with me, I wish I had a way to find out. That's why I set out to write this book. Adding to that was after dealing with the many misconceptions I've faced I wanted to dispel some of those and give a greater understanding as to what bipolar is. The most basic differentiation is that people with bipolar experience emotions in a much greater bandwidth. That range is between hypomanic and depressive emotional states which means your moods will fluctuate and you will feel things incredibly deeply, often painfully so. Triggers can result in a fluctuation of your emotional state.

Living With Bipolar is an insight into each of the main symptoms and emotions I experience with this disease and subsequently how I attempt to manage it. Each symptom is written in three sections.

Section one is literally what the symptom is to me. Section two is stream of consciousness, an insight into the thought patterns that occur inside that symptom. Section three is a short metaphorical section to describe the image of the symptom.

Michael Arvithis has done the artworks featured in the book. I approached Michael with the idea that I would write how each symptom looked to me and he would take that as a leaping off point to fully realise his version of that. His imagination, skill and talent are extraordinary. Michael's artwork brought a life to the book that words alone couldn't do. Outside of being an incredible artist he is a wonderful friend and I love him dearly.

In writing the book this way I'm hoping to reach all types of thinkers. If you're pragmatic, analytical or creative, the idea is to connect to you section to section depending on how you think. I wanted to give the reader the opportunity to empathise. If you don't have bipolar then it's truly impossible to understand what it's like. Even having bipolar it can feel like you don't understand it. Hopefully, in writing this way you can, even just a little. The pages to come are a step inside my mind.

- Xavier Coy

Depressive State

CRACK. POP. CRACK. The gentle rumblings of ice splintering ripple through your shivering legs. The wind howls across the ice with a bite so bitter you're squatting in a ball with arms wrapped around your knees to shield yourself. The freezing temperature has left you unable to register the sensations of coldness, it's just pain. Your head is bowed, eyes closed, unwilling to see what lays ahead of you. The wind intensifies and starts to shrivel the bones in your knees. If you remain squatting you may just freeze like that. You have no choice but to stand. You open your eyes to find yourself standing in the middle of a frozen over lake. It's just you, the ice and the skeletal trees in the distance. Light is fading fast.

Amongst the trees a flickering ember emerges. Safety. But how to reach it…You take a step and the ice fractures in every direction. You prod at piece of ice in front of you with your toe. It seems stable. Maybe the cracks are just sitting on the surface. A deep roar echoes around the lonely landscape. For a brief moment you feel heat from the all-encompassing fear. The ember dims for a moment. It's being whipped by the wind and at any second it could expire. You take another step and the cracks widen. Beside you a hole appears in the ice, just big enough for you to jump in. There's so far to go. Hope, all the way in the distance. How much energy you have in your legs and how much pain you can withstand?

Melancholia

The movie version of melancholia is someone sitting on a train wistfully looking out the window on a misty day. In reality it's pissing down outside and your shoes are soaked so you don't want to get off at your station because you're worried you'll get blisters. Your wistful look is just the look of someone who's immediately regretting eating a greasy kebab. Melancholia is gentler than some of its depressive cousins but no more fun. It's like being stabbed with a butter knife instead of a butcher's knife. In the recipe is a base of despondence mixed in with a dollop of dissatisfaction and a pinch of weariness. Everything is tinged with gloom. Motivation needs CPR. Self-doubt and pity have a strong heartbeat.

I should probably speak to someone. But what would I say if they asked how I am? Lie. Don't bother. You'd just bring them down. It's the middle of the day they're all at work anyway. Normal jobs with applicable skills. I wish I had skills. Or knew how to be useful. What if the toilet broke? I couldn't fix that. We'd need to get the plumber in. The plumber would come in all confident like 'I can fix this shitter' and I'd just have to stand there and say 'I don't have any skills sorry'. I bet you the toilet breaks today. Why would I wish that upon myself? If it happens, I've only got myself to blame now. I am a skill-less individual. Pop couple of words on a page. Cool. I wish I could make Mum proud. This, this - dark, slow, weak, ambivalent, tedious....Unclutter and clear your mind. Are you trying to Marie Kondo your fucking brain? She's got mad skills. I can't even do a deep house clean properly. This is what I am. I just have to live with it. A very insignificant and skill-less man.

It's the middle of a sunny day but it feels dark. You wander, groggy and numb like you're in a conscious coma with cool anaesthetic washing through your body like waves trickling into shore. You stub your toe hard and you stop, defeated. But there's no pain you just feel the recognition that pain should be there and that stubbing your toe was destined to happen. A glimmer of resolve appears in you to move. You have to act quick. It's not going to stick around. So you go to your calm spot, a peaceful little nook where the park meets the water. The water that normally feels peaceful now looks like it's moving lethargically. You can't help but feel that the sadness you've brought down has affected the water itself. Every push and pull feels like a barely beating heart. In the water is a glistening current. The water whispers for you to go and put your feet in. It promises to heal you. As you go towards it the current changes. You're left standing there watching the deceitful water as the anaesthetic swells. You stare in hope the current will change.

Not Enjoying Things You Used To

IMAGINE THAT YOUR entire life you've loved milk. You've loved milk so much that you could drink it with every meal. Set aside that it's a weird level of obsession for milk and avoid the Freudian take on it. You just really love milk. Then one day you wake up and the milk tastes different. You have another sip to be sure and same result. It's tart. Apply that to anything that gives you joy when depressive. Brightness, flavours, sensations and experiences are dulled or feel off. You set out to do things you enjoy every time without fail and…It fails. You're aware that this is that joyful thing but today, you're a witness. All you can do is run through the motions.

What puts a smile on your face? Let's do a happy thing. A smiley smiley thing. Go for a nice wander around the block and listen to a podcast. I mean it's not thrilling, is it? And I'd have to walk past that house that smells of cat shit and onions. Art gallery. There's that Sidney Nolan you love. The arid desert, the richness of the burnt oranges and reds. Why did I like this? It's swirls of colour mushed together. What even is it? What's art? Am I just here because I want to feel cultured? Everyone here looks like they just came from a hemp clothing outlet store. The Jackson Pollock. Art or gastro on a canvas? Probably put in the artist's label 'This represents melancholy as we search to understand the meaning of life.' WANK. Shoot the basketball. It's just a ball going through a hoop. Ridiculous. Watch 'The Office'. Everyone's so immature. At least I like my cute little house. Why though? The kitchen's tiny, the fridge goes in the laundry and it's poorly insulated. Ice cream fixes everything. It's…Ice cream is the exception to the rule. It's a bit sweet though. Everything else sucks.

You've arrived at a house you've created from all the different places you've lived, cherry-picking all the best bits of each one. You open the door and walk inside. Every pocket is a nostalgic dopamine hit. It's not glamorous but it's homely. You inhale deeply, all the wonderful memories attached to these walls should come flooding back but you're blank. As you move further in you see the walls are blackened with soot. You run your fingers across surfaces and feel the soft bed of mould blemish your skin. Faded memories blow towards you but they're fuzzy and you can only see shapes, colours and muffled sounds. This isn't home. This is a mockery of what you miss. You can hear the laughter from the memories but all you see is a grey cloud that passes through you like a ghost. The laughter swells and the clouds of grey circle around your head. As the memories start to reveal themselves, they disappear. It's just you and the empty house you don't know.

Inability To Accept Love

Spinning in a destructive chasm repeatedly thinking 'How could anyone love this mess?' Friends and family will tell you how much you mean to them but that's just what they have to say isn't it? Duty, guilt and pity have pulled people in close enough that they are unwilling to cut you off because they'd just worry too much. Love and care, it couldn't possibly be for you. Not only are you certain the relationships you have with people are fraudulent you are also convinced that at any moment they will all leave. So, what's the point in even allowing them into your world? It's self-loathing mixed with self-preservation.

I'm just a passenger here. Laughs all around and I'm here to pull the ripcord. Let that mirth explode into the atmosphere. We're only friends because we accumulated enough time spent together. Blind loyalty can only extend so far. Guess family will have to stay. Blood locked. People hate their families but still support them. I can see the pity look you're giving me. You know I'm cooked… That's why you're being overly nice. Yeah, that's the half-hearted 'I'm here for you smile'. That's the smile you give at a wedding of people you don't even like. Be aware, you stay here and you'll get sucked into the vortex. Thank you for trying. It's not your fault I can't be with you.

Out of the rich blue sky appears a solitary tiny flashing dot. You squint your eyes to decipher what it is but it does little to help. It moves a little closer and you see it's black and gold ball. It lasers is in on you. As it approaches you see the gold is fire, shards of flames are spitting into the air. The fire is warming the area around you creating a blanket of heat. This other-worldly structure is so magnificent you get the urge to reach out and touch it but instead you start retreating. It's there to protect you but you refuse to see the beauty anymore. Raging winds and pouring rain begin to fall but you're sheltered, it follows you as you back away. The ball has provided a cocoon around you. The safety it provides you leads you to gratefully rest your cheek gently against it but you're stopped. Your body has been loosely tied up with rope. If you really want to you can break free…The downpour intensifies as the flames start to die. You remain unmoved.

Lack of Self Worth

You've got the confidence of a Shetland Pony racing in the Melbourne Cup. What's at the forefront of your brain? That it's a shame you are the person you are. You're not good enough and never will be. You berate yourself with such enthusiasm it's as though it's almost a hobby. Every tiny detail of your person is under the microscope. You've never done anything worthwhile, never provided any positivity to anyone, never will. The worst parts about yourself, the parts you hate, that's you. Not even the kindest of words or gestures to others could convince you otherwise. You're the lowest of scum on the planet.

I'm toxic waste. I'm asbestos and cancer. Come near me at your peril. I wouldn't. I could disappear but leave you with the poison. I bet no one's thought about me in days. I'm just another number. A digit on the population counter. Nothing special. There are billions of people on the planet. The idea that everyone is unique is some bullshit primary school teachers started telling millennials so they wouldn't have to answer to pissed off parents. One in a hundred million is unique. You're not the one. And so many wonderful people get handed shitty cards, get sick, die young, me…I should take their place. That's fair. Even the ledger. I'm alive and that's it. Not nice or caring enough, not funny enough, successful enough, conscientious enough, ugly, fat, dumb, my dogs don't even like me. Easily forgettable.

You have been melted down to a thick sludge, spreading across the filthy ground as vulture like seagulls pick at you. Every peck feels like a dagger but your sludge like body just spreads across the Earth with no resistance. You're starting to turn to liquid and edge towards the sewer. If you fall in the putrid remnants of your body will dissipate into the ocean and leave a poisonous track, killing anything in its path. As you get closer to the drain suddenly your body reforms as a solid but it's not built back up to your former self. It's only solid enough to be swiftly pecked back down sludge. The seagulls rip in and pick you apart. With each furious peck they pull away the thin coating around your flesh to expose your raw insides to the elements.

Fatigue

This lethargy and weariness feels like it's set in for the season. Languid mornings bleed into lethargic evenings. You're in a body that's so heavy it's as though you have extra layers of skin you're lugging around. Coupled with a brain that's so slow it's operating on dial up internet in a 5G world, buffering and struggling to string two cohesive thoughts together. Seemingly, the only positive with being rendered so exhausted is the excuse to do nothing except all you wish for is vitality so you don't get to enjoy the nothing. Regardless of how much sleep you had you will roll through the day with a great big serving of lassitude. The day will be slow. Trying to fight it would be like trying to convince the dentist that you really do floss everyday.

Already I'm running on reserves. How can there be nothing from the beginning? You just have to push. Shame that requires effort. Maybe I'm sick. I've got chronic fatigue syndrome. Look that up. It'd make sense…Myalgic encephalomyelitis. Jesus Christ why did they call it that? I don't even have the energy to say it. Maybe that's what Jeff from the Wiggles had. He was a sleepy bastard. They really should've taken him to a doctor if he kept nodding off that easily. Okay let's not let the whole day go. Achieve something where I don't have to move. I could try listen to jazz to see if I can get what that's all about…What is this? These people need to chill out. You're chucking a bunch of crazy shit at the wall. That was too much I…I…Hugo Chavez drank over twenty cups of coffee a day. Maybe I do a Hugo.

Possessing a body so dense it houses bones made of steel, concrete cartilage and sand filled muscles covered in aluminium. You're down the bottom of a set of winding stairs. On an average day you're up and gone without raising a sweat. Today, this is climbing to the top of a lighthouse. With every step there is a crunch, a painful and tragic thump and zaps of electricity surge your brain temporarily cutting the power. Each breath is a reminder of how shallow it is, just reaching the top of your lungs. A needle pricks the top of your skull. You feel the pressure but no real discomfort. The air starts to leave your body as you deflate to the ground. Now, you're more cadaver than human. Despite how uncomfortable your crumpled up body on the concrete is you're happy to call this home for a little while.

Uncontrollable Crying

It's the battle between body and mind. Both can win. Physically, even with a clear mind, tears will roll down your face. All you know is that you're crying and it feels like it'll never stop and you can't recall whether there was even anything to start it. Mentally, you're on a knife's edge. Out of nowhere the dam walls can turn to dust. Any tiny thing can serve as a trigger. 'How are you?' is so loaded that you may as well be being asked about the saddest funeral you've been to and they begin to roll. Your body gets hot and your head throbs and you become exhausted. This must be a release, right? Surely this means you've got it all out? All it feels like is you desperately need to sleep.

If it starts then I'm screwed. I'll be chasing - I'm begging you to just… If I close my eyes then they can contain the tears. Give me a second to understand why…I'm sad, miserable. I guess? But it doesn't have to be this. Let me be numb. No, no, no…Just like that, huh? Tears are evidence that this pain is real right? This is tangible, concrete, undeniable despair. Salty. Maybe I should put on Schindler's List and really double down on this shit. When I'm so dehydrated and I've literally run out of fluid that'll kill it. I could do without the burning throat and stabbing in my ribcage but beggars can't be choosers. Pointless asking…Can we give it a break now? A breath. Exhale. Nothing. Dreaming is a dangerous thing. How long before I've recharged?

A single weed amongst a garden of ivy. You search for the root to pull it out. Dig and dig and…Found it. You rip the weed out. It comes out with a labyrinth of interconnected roots and removing it has sprouted another one. Two. They multiply. You rip and rip. You're clutching a mountain of weeds. There's a pause in time as if you're being given free rein to defeat them. Rip, rip, rip, until there's just raw Earth. It's over. As you turn to go you feel a tickle on your leg. A weed is climbing up your body. You reach down to pull it off and out of the corner of your eye you see green. The ground is now a forest of weeds. They have joined together to form an enormous wall. You are surrounded and overpowered.

Appetite

The human body is remarkable. Cells, muscles, organs, all perfectly constructed to create us. Some of us can run a marathon or swim the English Channel. Some of us can throw a really heavy ball from our neck in the most boring idea for a sport ever. Seriously, why is shotput a thing? And some of us when we're in a depressive period can eat so much, we feel sick but still soldier on. Your appetite is not only physical but it takes over your brain. You start thinking about food immediately after you've eaten. You justify how you need to eat more. You do everything you can to occupy yourself in order to stop going to the kitchen and nailing every morsel of food that's in the house.

You need to eat in order to survive. This is purely me continuing my life. Salad. Nice try mate. Yeah I'm mating myself cause my guts are pissed off. I need to gorge myself. Let's get Augustus Gloopy up in this shit. Ohhhh baby let me eat. This is a session now. Put me a table with Biggie, 70's Elvis and King Henry VIII and they'll all tap out before me. My body will have to shut down to make it end. I'm a glutton for gluttony. Shove. It. In. My. Mouth. Portion sizes are ridiculous. Who's opening a block of chocolate and not eating the whole thing? I'm so full. A fatty, fatty, full fatty. But I can't stop. I won't stop. Can you get diabetes after one night? Pump the insulin in I'm going back for more. Whatever the neighbours are cooking smells like soggy gooch but I'll take a plate if it's going.

A canyon so deep you only see black down below. The rocky landscape is so dry you can hear the rocks creak like they're calling out to you. A drop of rain falls and upon hitting the surface it fizzles. Steam flies into the air. Heavy set clouds converge above. Raindrops, heavier now, start launching down. Despite the mass of rain hitting the canyon it continues to fizz and disappear. The hissing sound of steam sounds like the canyon is in a rage. The surface is as dry as a bone. Suddenly the clouds thicken, grow and turn coal black. A thunderous downpour ensues. The rain is so thick you can barely see right in front of you. If there were houses below this downpour would surely sweep them away such is the force. Then, just as fast as it came, the rain stops and the clouds dissipate. The canyon begins to creak once again. Dry and angry.

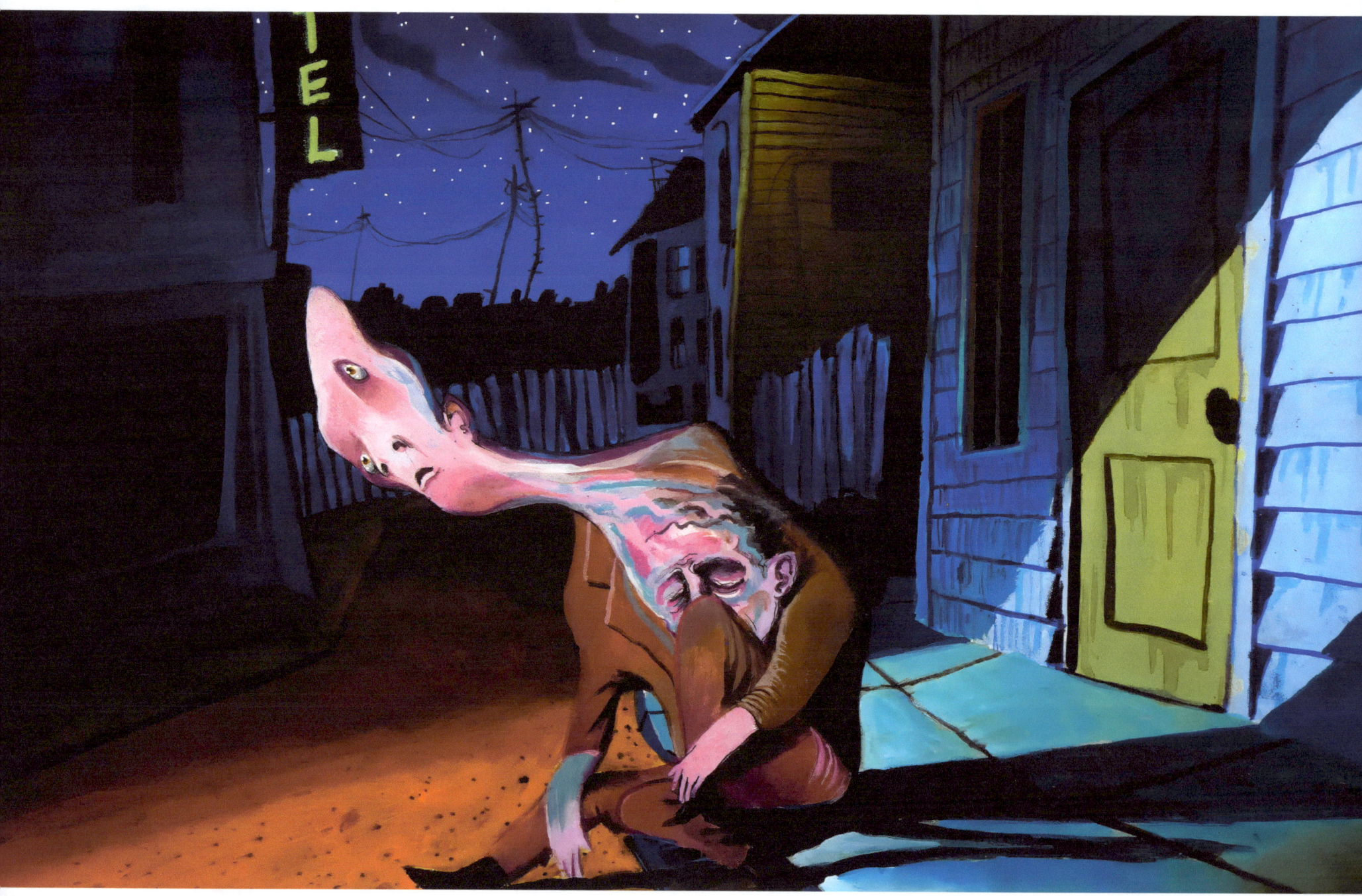

Hopelessness

Filled with such pronounced demoralisation that the thought joy could ever appear that you can't even begin to search for answers. This is going into a meeting with Jeff Bezos to ask for decent working conditions for Amazon employees. In every waking moment all you can find is pessimism, you look for quick fixes because anything that takes too long feels out of reach. There's nothing but suffering in your line of sight. You are tunnel visioned towards agony. The standing eight count finished hours ago. You have no will to fight. Disaster feels like a fait accompli. The only expectation you have for your life is that it's just going to beat you down further until you're a shell of a human with no escape. In fact, in this very moment, it feels like you already that way.

You broken brained…This, not this again. I told you that if you came back that I'd…Maybe this is the last time…No, I, I swear it's meant to give me a signal, a little warning flicker so I could up some resistance but it just fucks me sideways from nowhere. Why do you always do it like that? Why can't I just have something to protect myself? Maybe one day you'll achieve something amazing and you'll never feel this way again. Don't put that idea in your head. You'll just be disappointed. At what point is enough enough? Check myself into a facility. Admit that it's all too much. Pump me so full of numbing medication that I spend my days functioning without living. Cause that's what's coming. There's no point to anything. It lingers. I can't keep fighting. There's nothing to fight for.

Stranded in a desolate and abandoned town with no electricity, no signs of life, seemingly no way out. You spot a carcass ahead. If you don't find an escape you'll die. So, reluctantly, you try. With all your energy you heave yourself up. You barely rise before you slump back down. The bones in your legs have crumbled, unable to take the weight of your body. Defeat cascades over you like a sheet of shame. It's getting darker and darker. All that's guiding you is the stars but they're so dull they do little to light the way. In a desperate attempt to spark them into life you reach to the heavens. You grasp at the stars, pleading them to brighten. Your arm begins to shake with exhaustion despite only being above your head for a moment.
As your breath is expelled from your body your soul is dragged into the sky. With all the energy that's left in your body you attempt to follow. As you stand your bones turn to dust. Now, rest and wait. Wait for the morning sun to change the tune.

Misery & Despair

The last straw. It's when you hear the words 'I love you' and realise that they're just a cover to hurt you and make the other person feel better about themselves. Drenched in hurt and pain so extreme that you obsess over the idea that no one else has ever felt an emotion this devastating. This is suffering at its highest peak. You are an island, separated from the world around you. No words, no activities, no people can take you away from this feeling. The creature comforts you rely on are mere reminders of how unhappy you are. The outside world is unnoticeable. Cross the road when a car's right in front of you, a fight breaks out, a naked clown is blowing up balloons shaped like famous dictators…You don't see it. Happiness feels like it's locked away in Fort Knox and you've been given a toothpick to break in. You wish you could trade in your life for anyone else's. You are broken. Mangled. Pulverised. Alone.

Why am I even awake? It's meant to be a beautiful day. Don't cry. The day has barely started. What constitutes a beautiful day? Sunny? But you get burnt. So, it's not that beautiful, is it? It's harmful. Skin is just a surface for cancer. I deserve to have cancer. I'd look shit bald but them's the breaks. The Rock looks good. Yeah, cause you'd look exactly like The Rock. I'm pretty sure underneath my hair is a horribly misshapen lemon looking thing. Outside is dangerous. Inside is dangerous. Do I…What do I…? Do I try see what's out there? No. There is literally only one good temperature and that's twenty-three degrees. It's twenty-four. Everything other than twenty-three is tragic. Yes, tragic. The weather, could you be any more boring? Is this what you've become? I swore boring was the one thing I'd be never yet…Here we are. Stab me in the heart. It's barely beating.

It's pitch black and in the depths of a dense forest. Trees tower above, angled, encroaching in on you. They're a testament to nature's beauty but now they look intimidating and overwhelming. At any moment they could fall and crush you. Maybe they will. It you're lucky enough they will. A gentle wall of heat hits your skin. You spin, brow furrowed in search of the mysterious explanation. Light on the ground is seeping through the base of the trees. The light explodes into an inferno. The trees blow up in flames. Smoke billows out around you. Your lungs start to fill with poisonous air. You're coughing with the force of your entire body. The fire is growing. Flames rage around you. There are pockets to escape but you're exhausted and sick to your core. The fire's catching you quickly. Do you run and risk the burns or stay and be burned alive? The hairs on your skin start to singe. You remain. Breathless.

The Middle Ground

In the centre of an enormous citadel is a room that you'd expect to be grandiose but none of the trappings of luxury are there. It's bare, no furniture, only you and the infrastructure. The materials must be expensive but somehow feel cheap. There are slick marble floors, floor to ceiling glass walls on each side and an ornately carved wooden ceiling. The floor is so polished moving an inch will cause you to slip so you tense every muscle in your body to remain standing. A droplet lands below, another, there's a little pool at your feet. It must be sweat from the tension?

The wooden roof creaks, like it's moaning. You look up and see that the wood is swollen and moist, the cause of the droplets. It's rotting away rapidly, likely to cave in at any moment. After losing focus your legs begin to wobble. In order to avoid crashing to the ground you manage to lower yourself to your hands and knees. A chunk of the wooden roof lands beside you. In the corner of the room, you see the way out. There's a small door, just big enough for you, carved into the glass. You slide your way across the marble. Chunks of wood land beside you as you edge towards the door. You open it and a trickle of light hits your face. On the lawn outside are all your favourite belongings set ablaze, a fire ascending into the clouds.

Sleep

Depressive

An open bar to an alcoholic. There's an unquenchable thirst for unconsciousness. How many hours can you sleep? Days could pass it would still feel as though you've been deprived. You lust for the darkness, you lug yourself about only waiting for the time you can close your eyes. Every ounce of your body becomes glued to the mattress. Sleep is the avoidant solution put forward by your depressive brain to dodge the powers of depression. You'll just coast over it if you sleep through it. When you stir part of you feels guilty you've been in bed for so long that you're wasting the day but you're quickly asleep again. And when you're asleep you're in the deepest of sleeps imaginable.

Jesus Christ is it that late? Or early? I fell asleep at…I don't remember when. The sun was down. Or going down. So maybe it's been twelve, thirteen, fourteen…Bears hibernate for months. Maybe just a couple more. My brain's not ready, it needs rest. My eyes refuse to open. These sheets are made of lead. My body's aching. Getting up would be bad for my health. I need this rest.

A few weeks back I only got, like, five hours so I've probably got sleep debt. What kind of sadistic asshole came up with the alarm? I…need…this…one…more…hour…

With all your might you attempt to sit up. The light pouring through the window pierces your eyes. Time has frittered away yet you yearn to slump back down into the mattress and waste away some more. You rub your eyes gently. The skin on your hands feels softer than usual. It's wrinkled…Before you know it you are unconscious. Stiffness in your body is the only reason you wake. The light shining through has faded. Guilt pushes you to rise but as you stand you feel a weakness in your legs. You balance yourself. It's strange how weak you feel. You turn and face the mirror. As you look to the mirror you see that the wrinkles are ubiquitous. Your whole body is weathered. Old age has descended upon you. Days have rolled into one. Time, it's disappeared.

Hypomanic

Sleep when you're manic is like asking NRL players to have a headline free summer. You can go with hours of sleep over a period of days. You lay there and wonder whether you'll ever sleep again. You toss and turn with your eyes prized open. It's frustrating and defeating. When you can't fall asleep it leads to your brain ticking over and you can become anxious very quickly. So maybe you get up and do something to pass the time or exhaust yourself. Hopefully that flicks the switch and you doze off. Some nights your brain won't flick it. You're wired and edgy and you will be tomorrow too.

Let's get tandem here old brainy brain. My body is calm. Now it's your turn. No? Fine. Maybe I should concuss myself. Give me four hours. Three? I'll settle for three you slippery bastard. Is this bed made of woodchips and pebbles? Lay on your back. I've never fallen asleep on my back. I'm in a bed not an open casket. Side. This is alright. This feels good. Nope. Stomach. Shift. Again. I'm kicking my legs about like a bloody baby. Except babies sleep. Little fuckers. Showing off with your sleep. At least I don't shit my pants. Yeah this isn't a dude that's drifting off is it? Close your bloody eyes. I've done that. Try again. Maybe we've just been led by, like, society to believe we need sleep but really, we don't. Sleep. If I say it enough maybe it'll happen. Sleep. Futile bullshit.

Armed with only a pickaxe you're in the depths of a mine in the search for anything of value. From above you're only the size of a five-cent piece on a highway. With no clear place to start you rotate through your hips and swing wildly, hitting nothing. You raise the pickaxe above your head and bring it down into the surface with supercharged strength. A small amount of dirt dribbles away and a puff of dust wafts into the air. You wrench the pickaxe but it remains fixed. You've yanked with such force that when your grip loosens you fall to the ground. Pissed off and covered in filth you kick the pickaxe. The handle snaps leaving only half left. You yank, tug and bash the axe in a furious bid to set it free. Finally, the dirt loosens and the axe falls to the ground. With only half a handle to work with you give the most awkward and trying almighty blow to the surface. It ruptures the seemingly impenetrable Earth. A shimmer appears beneath a crack. You hack away but the axe splinters and falls to pieces, disappearing into the cracks. You scratch, claw and rip away at the Earth and finally you reach the shimmering object. A diamond…No, a five-cent piece. You continue to claw.

Memory Loss

Surreal and befuddling, being unable to recall memories kind of makes you feel as though you're going a little mad. People can remind you of anecdotes, hilarious or heartwarming, nothing. It's like you're hearing all these stories for the first time despite being there. Strangely, there are positives. Your brain has managed to wipe certain, not all, in fact you wish it'd wipe many more, but some painful and traumatic memories from your life. It serves as a protective mechanism. Although, these suppressed memories can be triggered and randomly appear with brutal consequences. This little cerebral quirk isn't isolated to yesteryear. Your short-term memory can also be distorted. It's easy to forget what you need to do or things you're meant to have done have totally disappeared.

Did I buy yoghurt? Or coffee? Well I have coffee. Both was a long shot. Shit did I call Mum back? Where's my phone? I'm meandering around the house like a geriatric looking for a blueberry muffin. Am I meant to meet up with someone? Am I lonely? Lonely…When there was no way out. I'm not going to hit you back. Stop. Please. I thought we let this die. The blood on the sheets. Then it…Goes black. Three missed calls from…Mum. I was supposed to call you back! That time we ate crab? I don't like crab. I liked the crab? Then we went where? Laugh along. Pretend you know what the fuck she's on about. I can hear what you're saying. I can imagine the context. The words are painting a picture. It's guesswork though. It's not like I – I mean I don't even know what day it is. Sounded great. Whatever night that was. Wish I was there. Three hits…We were at home and you were at the pub.

From the top of your skull, you feel a strange vibrating sensation. A buzzing starts in your ears. You close your eyes and shake your head in order to clear the maddening feeling. A bell rings and a card flashes up in front of you. 'Remember the colour for infinite wealth.' Blue. The vibrating recommences. There's a tickle in the back of your throat. You cough and you spit out pink goop. A dizziness overcomes you. Your eyes roll into the back of your head and you're looking up at your brain. It's turned to paste. All of your body has become soft clay. You raise your hands to your skull and press against it, pushing through the soft shell. With your doughy hands you attempt to reshape your mushy brain to its former state. It's slippery, the paste, though you manage to shape a respectable version. The bell rings. Your eyes spin back to the front of your head. The card. Your brain is mush. Yellow.

Avoiding Eye Contact

Depressive

THERE'S PRESSURE ON you to avoid eye contact at all costs. If they catch your eye then they might be able to see the sadness. If you get the sense they do then you'll burst into tears. Even a millisecond too long and your eyes become misty. This is protecting yourself with everything you've got. You can hide your misery pretty well on the outside but it shows in your eyes. Your eyes feel like they're rolling in slow motion. You look down a lot. It's less effort. Divert, don't let them see.

Unfocused, fuzzy, staring at nothing. I have to attempt to connect. At least acknowledge. It's rude not to. Your mother gave you manners. Glance. A moment. Blinking feels slow. Twenty-twenty vision and it feels like you're looking through mist. I've never noticed my blinking till now. Gravity has a hold on my eyeballs. It's tiring. I've spent too long staring down. Eyes. Flick up. Not a look. That was too close. You're staring down again. If it was a work of art you could get away with it but it's your own feet. This back and forth, to them and away, it's tedious, lugubrious. Flick up. Not look. Flick! Bail out! Did they see it? They saw. Welling up. Eyes. Flick. Busted. Pinch your eyes to stop the tears. I'm sorry. I wish I could see you.

Hypomanic

Darting back and forth like two coked up ping pong players. When you're manic and trying to avoid someone's gaze it's simultaneously conscious and subconscious. Consciously you know that because you're manic your engine is running hot and what goes up must come down. It's about not letting them see that the change is coming. However, subconsciously you are looking around the place because your energy is so high and your focus is so low that you almost forget to communicate with your eyes even if you're in the middle of a conversation. You hope that you're able to do this subtly but really you know your eyes are scanning everything and can't focus on one thing.

They're vibrating, my eyeballs, zipping around like a bucking bull. Eyes bouncing. The room is flashing by. Look at the wall. What's that? A cockroach? Are there other – there's one. I'll spot them all. Back to them. You're in the clear. Dancing eyes. Why are there so many cockroaches? They're fast. Hunt them down. Look at their ear. It's close enough to their face that it registers as eye contact. That can't be right. If someone started looking at my ear I'd be pretty weirded out. Their mouth. That's kinda intimate. Don't do that. Nose. Good. Stare at their nose. Funny little nose. I think they're seeing the surging. Where's the cockroach? Find the creepers. Ear. Mouth. Eyes. Nose. Funny little nose. What's up there? This ceiling needs a paint job. Bouncy boy eyes.

Blistering wounds around your eye socket. Blood is pouring out. You feel the damage but can't know the extent. Your eyes are spinning around trying to see what's happening. Blood continues to pour as an avalanche of rocks starts raining down on you.

The wounds around your eyes make it difficult to look up. You duck and weave but you're being pelted from everywhere. Every second dozens of rocks crash into you. Still, you duck and weave, circumventing not confronting. One enormous rock ploughs into you, knocking you to the ground. You close your eyes and hope it stops. It doesn't. Rock by rock you're getting buried alive. You open your eyes and look up. Suddenly the rocks stop. They are fixed in the sky, each one as if they're glaring at you. As you blink, they drop towards you then stop when your eyes open. They stay fixed as long as you do.

Anger

You are feeling hot with the bottled-up pressure of containing an explosion. Is it inwards or outwards? Both. You're a hungry toddler in an adult body in the worst sequel to 'Big' imaginable. You are pissed off at what you haven't done, what you have done and what you have to do. You're furious with yourself over nothing. Everyone around you is a problem waiting to occur. You create scenarios where you get involved in some conflict and give a withering and outrageously satisfying tongue lashing to someone. Minor inconveniences are cataclysmic. Getting cut off in traffic is like they've written off your car and sped off. Your fuse is short. So are your responses. Any tiny thing and you can crack the shits.

Where is it? Come on you cosmic cock. Where's that random thing that's there just to piss me off? Rain down on me with your bullshit world! When people do that thing – the thing – the thing that's just the most irritating – I don't know what it is now but someone's going to do it and I'll know then. And when it does they'll just – I mean why would they even – what the fuck am I doing? You're a dick. We're all dickheads. People are assholes. No one cares about anyone. People were stockpiling toilet paper in COVID. That's how little we care about people. We don't even want our neighbour to enjoy a shit. So fuck them. And fuck you for needing their approval. You need to shut up and get on with your life. Why are you so pissed off with everyone else? You're the problem. Sort yourself out mate. Jesus Christ. Put some effort into not being a raging prick. Hey. You. Get. Away. From. Me.

The keys have been handed over to you. A tank full of ammunition is at your disposal. Without thinking you jump in and start the engine. It's infuriatingly slow. You bash at the controls, wanting it to roar into life like a formula one car. You drive down a crowded street, scraping and smashing through the cars next to you. People are around, you try your best to avoid them but there's only so much you can do. If someone's collateral damage they had their chance to move. A person stands in front of you. Not running away or diving to safety, this person stares the tank down. Now's your chance. Your finger hovers over the button to blast. But you can't bring yourself to fire. The tank rolls up close to the person and comes to a halt. You see out and notice that the person is you sporting a wry smile. Sweat is dripping all over your body. You fire a hail of ammunition into the sky.

Unwanted Thoughts

The randomness and ugly nature of these thoughts keeps you off kilter. Your brain terrorises you with such disgusting and distressing thoughts you don't even recognise yourself. They're designed to make you feel pained, putrid and unhinged. These thoughts are so pernicious they have a lingering quality that pleasant thoughts don't. There's nothing helpful, nothing positive, nothing rational, nothing conducive to happiness here. Rapidly you find yourself agitated, anxious, angry, sorrowful, worthless and I hate to say it…Mental. You can't escape it. They come in a flurry and snowball quickly. Expect a heavy series of painful blows before they leave.

What would happen if I kicked a kid in the head? Not hard. Just a tap. Would I go to jail? The fuck was that? What's wrong with me? Where do I begin? You think you're smart but you're just good at hiding your stupidity. You're a pain in the arse. You bring up that your former high school was a paedophile priest factory too much. I reckon we had a suss one. The vibe of that bloke. Either really nice or too nice. I wonder if he's still out there. Oh god…I need to call the cops. If I don't and he – I mean how would I live with myself?

Is that a lump? Maybe I've got cancer. Is that a lesion? Maybe it's HIV. How could I have HIV? Cause Magic Johnson had it and you watched the doco so you probably have it too. So because Magic Johnson has it I've got it? Shit do I have it? No. I don't have HIV. Just cancer. You should kill yourself. You've definitely got cancer so…What's the point? Kill yourself.

Hairs are being individually plucked from your skin by an invisible force. The first series of plucks come from your arm. You go to rub it, hoping to relieve the discomfort. Before you can another hair is plucked from your back. So, your attention turns to your back. You try in vain to reach but there's more plucking elsewhere. It's gathering momentum. Your toes, your eyelashes, your arse. You don't know where to look. The discomfort is so severe that your entire being begins to shake. There's not a single hair left on your body. A yelp like a wounded dog blurts out of you in a manic plea to ward off whatever is causing the pain. With no hair left to pull the raw skin on your body is the target. Now, with little fight left you're left trembling as your skin begins to rip away from your body.

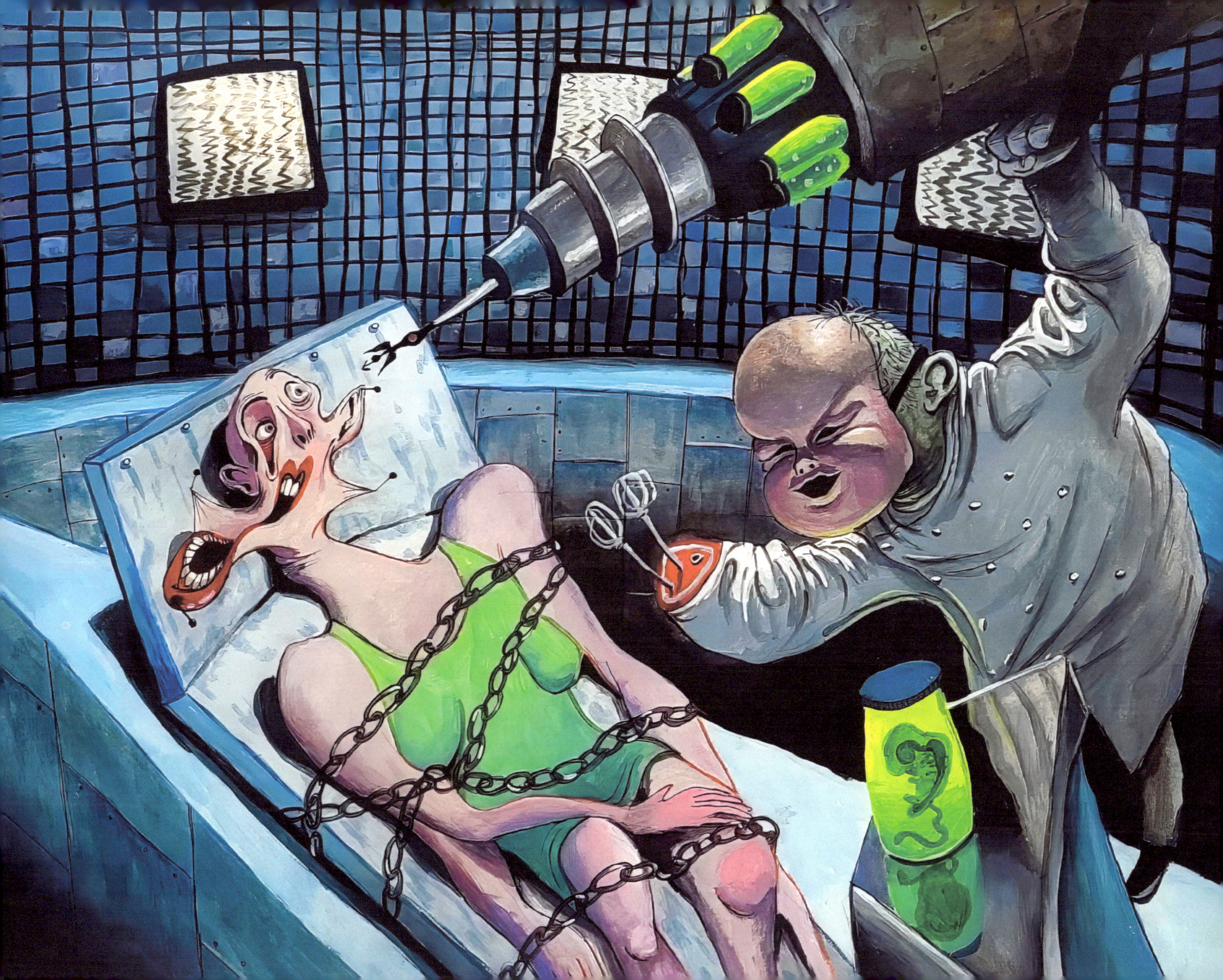

Shamefulness & Regret

You've saved up all your money to buy a Mercedes. You've got a wedding coming up so you buy a Hugo Boss suit. You're in the mood for something sweet so you grab a Fanta. Then you come to learn that car was driven and the suits were worn by the Nazi's. The Fanta's safe though, right? Nup. Invented in Nazi Germany. Nice one you bigot. In times of the greatest suffering that's so torturous it curdles your blood you'll find shame and regret. You find yourself reaching into your past and dredging up moments you wish you did differently or moments you embarrassed yourself. These memories feel so immediate they feel like they're happening in front of you. You're able to convince yourself that you are just your mistakes. There's an insatiable need to lambast yourself. Growth doesn't matter because you are destined to return to the walking mistake that you were. There's no way you can be the person you want to be. You are utterly disgusted with yourself.

Why can't I just wipe my brain? Why is all the painful stuff so clear? What a revolting mass of meat I am. But I'm kinder now. I know myself. I've got things under control. I'm more able to be the real me. I'm more than just the shit things, aren't I? But you had the chance not to do shit things and you did them didn't you? Idiot. Pig. I'm sorry. I can be better. To everyone. You're only capable of hurting people. Pissing them off. Infuriating and upsetting them. How could you ever forgive yourself? I've grown! No, not good enough. Bastard. And you've only got yourself to blame. You will forever be the worst of you. The past doesn't fade. Luckily for you it brightens when you think you're better than you were. I'm… Pathetic. Just a corpse waiting to happen.

Off the highway is the most pitiful, filthy, revolting motel. Not even bed bugs would park up here but you… This is your life. Each centimetre of the place is tarnished with its own tale of sadness. The motel is a monument to loneliness where sorrowful souls come to loom. You're sat staring at your reflection in the bacteria ridden pool. It's deathly quiet. The smell of rotting flesh wafts through the air. It's so putrid that the air tastes dirty and on each inhale your nostrils quiver, your tonsils shake and a gag rises in your throat almost causing you to throw up. The other lost souls appear and disappear around you, never seeing you. Your shoulders slump with misery and as your elbows hit your thighs, they slip out from under you. You realise that the rotting flesh smell is your own. It's been slowly falling away from your bones. Seeing what you've become makes you recoil so hard your body shakes and you slide face first into the pool. The bacteria nibbles away at your rotting body as you sink to the bottom.

Lack of Control

A SELF-APPOINTED "ALPHA MALE" in a gym supplement store. When your bipolar is undiagnosed, untreated and unmanaged your life is dictated by whatever emotional state you are strapped into. With that comes terror. You don't know where the day will take you emotionally. Any shift in emotion is too quick to catch. You're paranoid, afraid and miserable. You go from sad to destroyed, worried to panic attack, teary to fury. You're fixated on just trying to be okay and not a complete mess. On the mornings you're lucky enough to wake up feeling good you know that could change in an instant. On the mornings you wake up anxious or depressed you know it's going to get worse and you're in for a fight to get through the day just to fall back asleep. You're barely able to function like a normal member of society. The emotions are just too overwhelming. You feel damaged beyond repair. That ambulance driving past…It's for you.

Depressive

You don't stand a chance. This life is kinda funny isn't it? How fucked up miserable it is. The world is staring you down, backing you into a corner. Curl up. If you have to talk to anyone keep your words to a minimum. Keep it tight. Keep it together. I'm a ticking time bomb. There's only one way to end it…Get a coffee. Rudimentary and habitual. Achievable. Why are there tears welling in my eyes? Get to the street. No one here. Good. But maybe if there was someone here I could talk to them. They could see you're in pain, they could help. My head feels heavy. My eyes are falling into my skull. My brain is turning to puss. My heart wants to stop. All this relentless – all the swatting away of the muck… Someone's coming towards me. I think I know them. Walk. Any direction. The world is black. I'm on my own. Dangerous thing.

Hypomanic

My breath it's – I can't breathe. You can. Just slow it down. I can't! Slow. What happens if my chest collapses into itself? There's too much energy in your body. Expel it. I can't catch them – thoughts – they're running wild – head spinning on its axis. Fire spitting in my brain. I can't take – I can't do anything. My chest – it's cramping. Oxygen. I need more oxygen. Tick. Tock. Tick. Tock. Breath's getting shallower. Breathe. Sad state of affairs when I have to tell myself to breathe. Why are you looking at me? My reflection. Shit. I can't do this. What if I stay like this forever? Move. Tap your fingers. I'm just holding on. That stabbing in my solar plexus…Panic. Raging through me. I don't want to hurt anyone. Can't contain the panic. Run.

An entire stadium watches you stand nervously in the middle of a boxing ring. You've never thrown a punch before but your hands are wrapped and you're in there to fight. The only problem is that instead of being matched up with one opponent you're faced with one in each corner eagerly awaiting their turn. They're bouncing on their toes, eyes wide. You get the choice to pick your first combatant. The smallest one. Step forward, hands up, shift around so as not to be hit, punch thrown. Miss. They're laughing at you. The warrior in the other corner jumps forward and thumps you in the back of the head. Dazed, you're hurled towards your intended pugilist. The boxer to your left wallops you across the jaw. As you stumbling about, barely conscious, the last of the fighters raises their arms as if to hug you and keep you safe. You extend your arms to accept their kind offer and they deliver a crushing blow to your rib cage. Breathless and beaten you dive to escape under the ropes. All four pin you down. The beating intensifies. Blood explodes into the air. They'll decide when they've had enough.

Hypomanic State

The edge of a cliff, high above the ocean. Despite the precarious position you're in it's hard not to acknowledge the sheer resplendence of the outlook. The waves are choppy yet somehow tender. When they thump together it looks like a dance. When they rise to their apex it's as if they're kissing. The whole ocean, in all its chaos, is united and glorious beyond words. The swell intensifies and now when the waves surge, they look like brawling lions in the wild. Misty sea spray floats into the air. You close your eyes and breathe in the air. When you open them, you've been transported into the sky. Surprisingly you feel no sense of panic. You're overcome with glee and excitement.

It's doesn't stay long. Like a plane that's engines have failed you plummet ferociously towards the sea and plummet into the ocean. Injured but alive, you sink deep beneath the surface. At first you wait, hoping you'll reach a point where you begin to float. Panic sets in and you thrash about underwater. Oxygen is fading as you see the light blue of the surface way above. Your limbs are flailing, your lungs feeling like compressed sponges and your head is filled with so much pressure it could explode. You desperately thrash your arms and legs, you rise and make it. Just. The clifftops, previously a glorious beacon of beauty, are now an image of deceit. It's time to swim. Only you can rescue yourself.

Anxiety

Pretend you're happily riding a bicycle. It turns into a tandem and a three hundred kilo powerlifter jumps on the back. Now we're going whatever way big boy wants to go. That big boy is anxiety. Anxiety is one of the emotions that typically sits in hypomania but can quickly send you to depressive. Such a malleable little asshole aren't you anxiety? Anxiety claws away at what's real and distorts it. In previous years you were a colossal asshole who no one liked. Today you're waiting to be attacked by some external force. And your own brain. Tomorrow is laced with problems that are certainly fake. If you're stressed you can catastrophise so badly it cripples you. This goes in an express cycle. It goes. It comes back with renewed vigour. Threat is everywhere. Panic is leading the dance.

The roof could fall in at any second. Crash down and cover you in bricks. Cute dog. What if it attacks me? Can you get rabies in Australia? Is that how I die? Foaming at the mouth on the side of the road. Why is that person standing there? Why is he alone? Is he dangerous? He could be a psychopath. Hide in plain sight. What if he looks at me? Have I done something wrong? Do I need to apologize? Run. If you run then what's around the corner? The police? Why are they there? What did I do? I'm just standing here. That guy. He's not looking at me. Why isn't he looking? Does he hate me? Do I know him? Is he friends with someone who doesn't like me and they've spoken about me? Who doesn't like me? I'm sorry. Who does he know? I'm sorry. Who's the person that hates me? Everyone.

Your face is stretched, elongated, skin so strained you're no longer recognisable. The beating of your heart sends pulses up your throat and into your face, pushing the skin outwards. It has become the face of many faces. Thoughts attach themselves to the pulses and add power to them, stretching the skin further. The pressing thoughts begin to expand and combine into a cacophonous throbbing. Your head can't contain it all, they bounce, rattle around, there's no escape. The inside of your head like a broken pinball machine where the ball never dies. You feel like you're being watched from every angle. This ugly mess has nowhere to hide when you feel the eyes of the world peering. They see your internal engine, what you think, the emotions, judging all of it. A crowd of ghost's form around you to watch the grotesque pulsating head. They whisper to you but you can't make out the words. The sounds are terrifying enough.

Agitation

A FAILED STAND-UP COMEDIAN takes a seat at the table when the accountant tells a joke that cracks everyone up. How dare he…Stick to your numbers, number-boy. A nitrogen particle has the potential to become irritating. Macro to micro, everything's on the table. You're at the ready for how you can be annoyed or nervous. The insignificant can escalate to terribly worrisome and take far too long to recover from. Deep, deep inside yourself you are rumbling with pent up tension with no release valve. It's as though every muscle in your body needs to move at once but you're being forced to sit still. Even your hair follicles feel like they're stressed.

Stop tapping your foot. It's annoying me and it's my bloody foot. Fine. Tap. Tappitty tap tap. Shut up. Is that a fly? How'd that fly get in here? Can you at least have the decency to stop your buzzing if you're going to be here? Please don't land on me. I know where you've been and my family were convicts so I have a high probability of getting scurvy. Does dog shit cause scurvy? Just leave me alone. Why am I arguing with a fly? Why does this fly have such a superiority complex that he thinks he can just cruise on in here? That's so emblematic of this time in history. Narcissism is the flavour of the century. Tap. Stop! Get out fly! The fly doesn't know what it's doing, dickhead. Bye! Don't let the door hit you on the way out you inconsiderate asshole. That thing was kind of terrifying huh? I better not have scurvy. Just what I need.

Bugs. Crawling across your brain. Their little legs like pricking pins. You scratch your hair but the itch is below the surface. You dig your fingernails in so hard to your skull that you cut the skin. The scuttling of the bugs starts to frighten you so your scratching turns to shredding and clawing. You've used every bit of force in your fingers and arms. Your skull pops open, exposing your brain. Horror floods through your body. But the itch is just too much. You scrape and dig and the bugs look as though they're shrinking. You relax. The bugs are now smaller but faster. You realise that your fingernails have disintegrated and all that's left are nubs. Your heart begins to flutter as no solutions are presenting themselves. The itch continues.

Restlessness

You're Chris Rock waiting for Will Smith to call. Discontented and wobbly. Emotionally and physically, you are uncentred. Your brain hovers around in search for something to do or occupy you but quickly switches gears. Everything is boring or unimportant so you freeze with indecision. You should be doing something but what? Nothing arrives so anxious thoughts begin appearing. Focus is oscillating between locked into an idea and totally off the wall. You read a few pages of a book but suddenly the book is too long, the wrong genre and a waste of your time. You exercise but you forgot about the washing that needs to be done immediately for no reason. Every answer creates a new problem.

It's good for you to take some time to just chill out. You know me, a chill dude. Nothing but chill. I'm ready to chill. This is ridiculous. Chilling is not – it's not, like, a thing I like. Well, I like it when I like it and I don't like it now. What if I never work again? How much money is enough to feel comfortable? You don't have it. What if I need fifty-grand right now for some reason? Maybe I'll join the army training program, infiltrate from the inside and write a movie about it. How dull. Itch. My fingers are weirdly shaped. They don't even give a satisfying scratch. Who is the most famous person with four fingers? Instead of focusing on work you want to think about four fingered famous people? Come on. Come on what?!? What do I do?!? Hey, hey, it's not happening for you today. Why don't we try this chilling thing again? Little couch time. Try it. Nice, huh? Well nice while it lasted. You definitely needed to walk to the front door and back. Normal stuff. Was that weird? Am I weird? Front door and back. Front door and back.

A sprawling ant hill grows and grows in front of you. Ants are scurrying everywhere. You get flighty with the chaos of it. But, despite how chaotic they look, they're well organised. Yet all you see is the manic movement. While your eyes have been trying to find the leader, the hill has become mountainous. Ouch. Ouch. They're nipping at your heels like a rabid dog. You jump around and fall onto your back, becoming bait for their feasting. Hordes of ants are circling you as you thrash about to scare them off. One arm goes left and they feast on the right. You get back to your feet and run. As you turn all you see are ant hills spread across the land. You scurry to what feels like safety but you forgot to brush your legs. The ants have become glued to you. They're multiplying on your skin and travelling with you.

Inability to Sit Still or Focus

You know when you put a dog's food out but then a bird flies near it and the poor little bugger has no idea what to do? They're really hungry but they really hate birds. So, they lunge for the bird and instead step on their squeaky chew toy that they now have to destroy. Yeah. That's you. The best way to describe this is overstimulated. Rather than being frustrated with the situation you're just doing whatever you want to do in any given moment. You may sit for a moment but then you're up and you're pacing around. You've opened up thirty tabs on your laptop from the news to weird historical facts to YouTube videos of the opioid crisis in America to seeing how fast a wombat can run. All in all, you just kind of feel haywire, constantly asking 'Why am I doing this again?'

Focus. One thing. Uno thingo. I should learn another language. What though? Something out of the box. Turkish. Oi. Lock in. One. Thing. Dickhead. Emails. Five in your inbox. Crazy to imagine a world without emails. Five's not that many. Stupid uncomfortable chair. Why can't I learn to sit on the floor like they do in Japan? Japan's sick. I could learn Japanese. Is this chair really uncomfortable or do I just have a bony arse? I'm up. Gotta replace these chairs. Wait why did I come go into the bedroom? Wasn't I - emails. Working from home's no good. Too many distra – Café's much better. Mmm…Emails. I should only accept correspondence via carrier pigeon. I haven't sat still for a second. Everyone here probably thinks I'm some – why am I holding my phone? This bench needs cushions. Does this café not even care about their clientele's posterior? Why am I so concerned about the condition of my arse? I need to get new undies from K-Mart.

Dropped into the middle of the outback, vast and baron. You've been there for days. You're exhausted and starving. There's a kangaroo in the distance staring directly at you. You don't feel comfortable with the idea but it's your only way to eat…Hunt. Your life depends on it. The red sand tickles your bare feet. You feel a small incision on your calf. The bushes by your side are sharp and spikey. Specks of blood run down your legs. You wipe the blood but it smears. The kangaroo! Step by step. The sand tickling, the blood dripping, step by step. It starts to hop away towards the horizon. You run but sweat from your forehead drips into your eyes. You shake your head, the blood, you wipe your leg, the tickling of your feet. The kangaroo! It's gone…You whip around to find it but another bigger kangaroo is there standing a foot away from you. The sweat, the blood, the sand, the muscles in your hand tighten. Sweat drips in your eye, it closes, it opens again and the kangaroo hops away. You leap forward and miss, falling into the sand.

Frenzied Speaking

You're the Usain Bolt of chitter chatter. Speech as quick as this is such an obvious sign of hypomania you may as well hand people a business card saying 'Nice to meet you, I have bipolar' on it. The words are pinging off your tongue so quickly it's like you no longer need to breathe. Rapid, wild, almost unintelligible, you roll on and on. Your thoughts are chasing your mouth. There's so much to say but so little time. Words start to become jumbled and smooshed together as you race to get them all out at the same time. The person opposite you will just have to wait patiently to speak.

Wait, okay, okay, I have to tell you more about today, then tomorrow, this weekend, last week too actually, my opinions on various geopolitical matters I don't know enough about, sports I know too much about, this podcast I'm listening to - Scammers are, like, hectic. Wild shit. Everyone loves true crime nowadays huh? Is this just blah blah – can you understand me? This is a lot. You're not listening. Or maybe you are. I can't tell. Doesn't matter. You'll get your chance. You're spinning out. You think I'm crazy. That's okay. Crazy is interesting. People are so boring. Their turn. Had your chance. Did you miss that joke? Should I say it again? I may have rushed the punchline. They're not listening. Say something bizarre. There you go. So what if this shit's nonsensical. I said it. Hang on – one more thing. Well, this was great. Think I covered about one percent.

Your tongue has been pulled from your skull and is strapped to an electric car going around a circuit. Control, it's out of your hands. Rapid, barely visible, the car flies around the track. It's a blur. Sparks fly off the circuit, it flies around a bend, the electricity surges and WHOOSH! The car spins out of control and crashes into the wall. It somehow lands on its wheels, zips vertically up the wall and screeches across the roof. The car drops for a moment before shooting around the room. It's taken on a life of its own and pulling you along for the ride. You try to grab it but every time you get close the car crashes into your forehead and continues to jet around the room.

Risk Taking Behaviour

You're going for it. You're going to ask a full-blown narcissist to consider your point of view. Wild man. Vices, provoking challenges and rash decisions are on the menu in this do whatever you want reckless mindset. Actions come well before the thought is fleshed out and consequences come when you're back down on Earth. You have a thirst to elevate your heartrate and there's no time to waste. Life is meant to be lived so you will do it at its highest octane. No one ever got anywhere without taking risks so maybe you have to take a couple. Excited isn't good enough. You need adrenaline. Chances are you haven't even made it this sentence you're already off doing something you probably shouldn't. God speed.

Let's get pissed. Really pissed. Stupidly pissed. Black out pissed. Get a bag. Ket? Need fast cash. ATM. Nah. Fifty on horse 10. Dud. Do it again. Horse 11 this time. I'm not a sucker. Not falling for your game horsey. 12. I knew it. Drive. Fast. This shit's real. Damn that blood feels like fire. Deadlift a car. Break records. Or my back. I should get into the UFC. I'm fast. Fast twitch. This is speed. Pure speed charging through my veins. Dude, legend, send that asshole a blistering message telling him all the things that are wrong with him. I have to stand by my principles. Get a tatt! Oh! Get a tatt of Shannon Noll's goatee as a goatee. That's gold. I need the new iPhone. What? Where'd all that money go? Oh. Looks like I'm going to Frankfurt in a couple of days.

A gun in a mount is ten metres away from you. A machine clicks the trigger every few seconds. No bullets yet. There's no way of knowing whether there's any in the chamber. You stand perfectly still awaiting the answer. Click. Nothing. A dark chuckle trickles out of your body. You dare it to take another shot, spreading your arms like some sort of demonic angel. You're fast enough to dodge it. Click. A hearty laugh. A few metres to your left is a blindfold. Challenge accepted. You grab the blindfold and as you do – BANG! A bullet fires where you standing. With the blindfold in your hand, you have a choice…And you like your chances. You've got the reflexes of a yoga instructor flicking through a Lululemon sales rack. Not a chance you'll be hit. You stare down the barrel of the gun. Time slows, you dive to the ground just as the gun fires. You dodged it. This time at least.

Grandeur

Fuelled by a ridiculous heightened sense of your own magnificence. A work of objective mediocrity is your magnum opus. Pretty average is looking like a Pulitzer. Maybe they'll give you your lunch for free cause that's what they do for legends. Do the rounds of calling friends because you have some important perspectives that the world has not considered. You're the pilot over the PA, every word you say you think is of the utmost importance. Risky jokes you're convinced will land turn out to be a little too boundary pushing. The joke had to be told. And it was funny. Rogue but funny. You're ground breaking, Earth shattering and so bloody important.

The world needs me. I am like no other person that's ever existed. I'm not this stock standard, IKEA personality, beige bullshit. Off. Kilter. Wired, weird and wonderful. Cause I know I'm something special. My brain is different. It operates on a different frequency. And for those who don't see it yet – they're in for a treat. Cause when you see it you won't be able to unsee it. Your lives will change. You will invest, re-invest, be enamoured with me. Just you wait. But fuck waiting you have to see it now. You'll never understand the bipolar brilliance. Winston Churchill had bipolar and he got through a World War – we're in symbiosis – all of us in that one percent. The superpower that fuels us. It's tapped into something special. Brain's connected up to the supercomputer of the lizard people.

Now that's whack. I'm whack but thinking there's a group of lizard people running the world that's off your nut, punching cones for breakfast kind of gear. That's funny. I reckon I could get a giggle out of Putin. He'd probably want to put me in charge of the Kremlin. Needs my leadership. Sorry, Vlad, not my vibe. Cheers for the offer though.

Set in a medieval castle where being a royal means you sit amongst the Gods. The King has entered and everyone dives to kiss your feet. No one is on equal footing, the other beings are merely the peasantry. They should consider themselves lucky to put their lips so close to your skin. Your eyes sparkle with specks of sapphires, your footprints leave silver stains on the Earth and your breath smells of the finest perfume. An enormously long table is adorned with gold plated cutlery, fine china, immaculately clean, and food packed so high you can't even see the table cloth. People are lined up against the walls desperate just to sit with you but they can't. A crown is set upon your head. Diamonds, gold and jewels make this a relic of immeasurable cost. Yet the crown is so heavy you can't balance it. As you lean slightly to one side out of discomfort the crown falls and smashes into pieces. Scattered on the ground are all the fragments of the crown. The food is taken away and the people chortle as they leave. You bellow out and bash the table but no one listens.

Euphoria

It's got three-hundred views! Your freestyle rap video you put on YouTube is practically going viral. You must be Eminem. The most alluring and hazardous of the symptoms. This is where you're at the very peak of the positive side of mania. Serotonin feels like it's pumping around your body with every heartbeat. What goes up must come down and if not controlled then the crash is fast and brutal. But while you're up here… Nothing gets better than this. It's magnetic. This is the reason you look to lose the medication. If life was always like this, if you were always this 'on', this elated, exhilarated, then every second would be ecstasy. This is overly extra bright colours, sky high optimism and unbreakable confidence. Life is at its most wonderful and it's impossible to imagine that you were ever struggling.

See why would I get help? Your good moods go to ten out of ten, I get to thirty, forty, one hundred. Nothing will ever go wrong. It can't. The world around me is beautiful, stunning, dazzling. Oceans, rivers, lakes, trees, flowers and blue skies! How lucky we sit amongst it all. Mankind is spectacular too! Roads, cars, how?!? These steel cages on wheels that move across a hard surface that people made to transport us to where we want to go in a flash! That's magic. And how amazing is magic?!? What a beautiful level of appreciation I have for things. You're alright, Xav. My heart is open to the world. Why hold onto resentment? Don't waste a second of this on anything other than the beauty.

Every sinew of your body is radiating, massaging itself, a shield of oxytocin covers your skin. You have so much joyous energy you bounce around like a kid on Christmas morning. The bounce becomes so extreme you're catapulted into the sky. High amongst the clouds you release all that's weighed you down. The clouds embrace you like they've been waiting for you to arrive. You want to greet them all so you soar from cloud to cloud, embrace to embrace. Overcome with ecstasy you burst into gleeful laughter. Birds flying with you in sky start to cackle along with you. The clouds around you form chubby cheeked faces with wide grins. Lightning strikes you but it bounces straight off and your body becomes plated in gold. Cackles of laughter ripple all around the atmosphere. They build and echo so everyone down below can hear. You radiate such palpable joy that you create a shield around you. Nothing can harm you.

Energy

No, you haven't had fifty shots of espresso are pumped through a drip straight into your bloodstream. You're buzzed on your own engine. You're the psycho kid who's drank the red cordial and shovelled handfuls of sherbet into their mouth. You're as amped up as the seedy middle-aged man who finds out there's a discount going at his local "massage parlour". It's all systems go all day. Your brain is springing with activity. It's buzzing with ideas with no way of keeping up with them all. You run around all day you don't slow down. It's impossible to exhaust yourself. You're not an elite athlete you're just manic to the gills. You feel so light and tingly, zipping and zagging and not stopping.

Leaping, ducking, diving, levitating. Coffee. Caffeine on top of this? Shit yeah. Fly prick. Smashed it. Burnt tongue. Don't care. Shower. Bang. Showered. Record pace. I'm setting shower records now? Not dry. Don't have time. Clothes, keys, phone, door slammed in a flash. I'm racing against…There's nothing to race against. Well race something. Where to go? Anywhere. Hit it with pace. Saw all I needed to see. Would see again. Will see again. Get to it. Laptop. Oh my god are you seriously giving me that stupid spinning wheel? Piece of – good. Tap, tap, tap – ratatatatatatatat – keep up fingers. This is light work. Typos will be tolerated. Fix it in post. Fingers! You're killing me here! Get out of this joint. Run. Run faster. Spin bike. Work. TV. Settle. Spin bike. Work. Settle. Sedative. Extra sedative.

Your body has split into a million specks and coiled back together. You've ended up as a tiny speck of grease in the exhaust of a muscled-up car. You're stuck inside hurriedly trying to break free but you remained pinned against the metal. The engine roars into life, the rattle of the machine unshackles you. You ping around inside the exhaust waiting to be catapulted out into the air. The engine's humming and you start to growl with anticipation. The engine revs and the pace of the pinging intensifies. You're barely visible now you're moving so fast. You're bouncing around the exhaust with such force you're starting to dent the metal. The car bursts into life and flies away. The exhaust has thrust you into the air. Within a millisecond you are sent into orbit. There's no catching you.

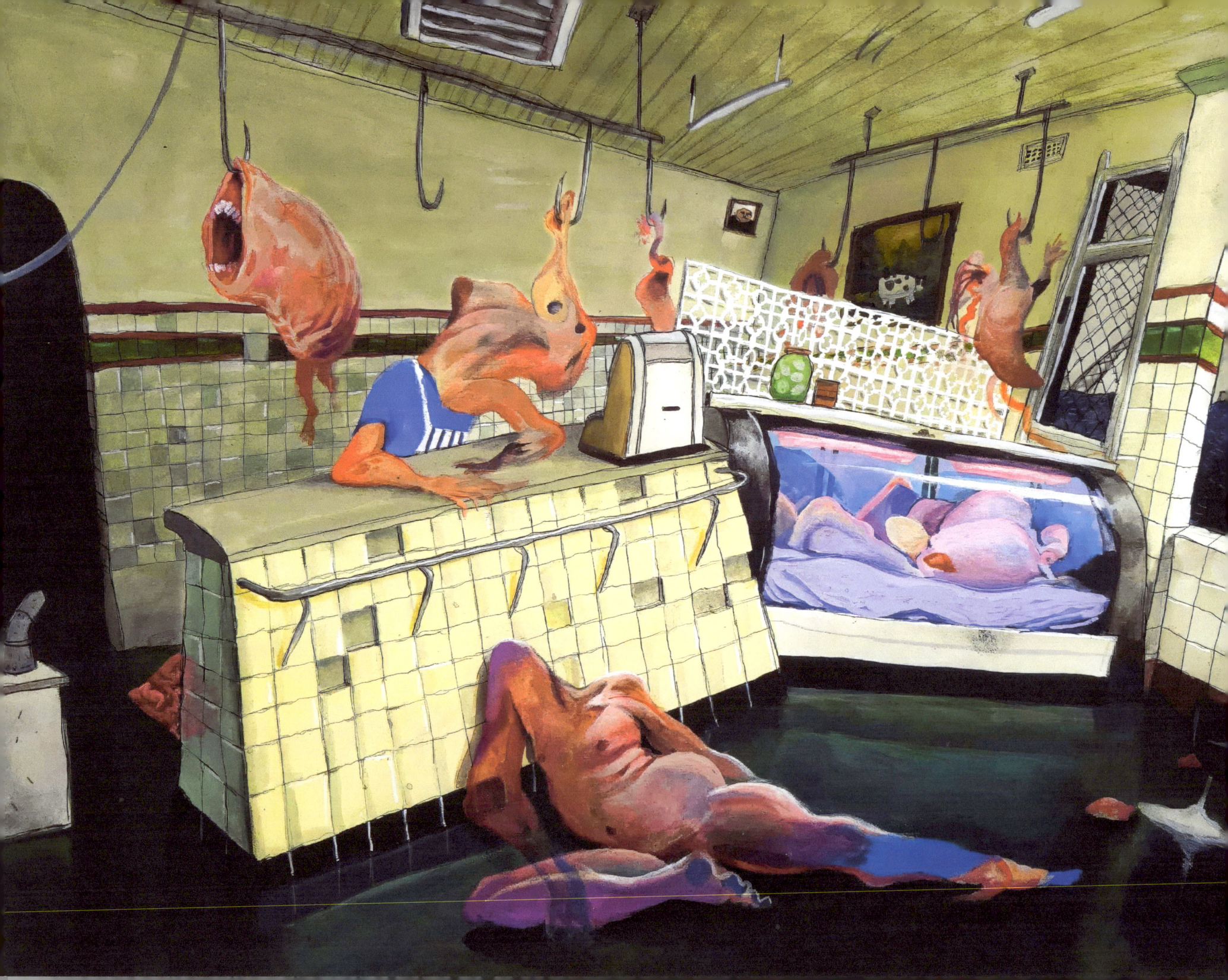

Disorganised Behaviour

THE TICKETEK SYSTEM when Taylor Swift tickets go on sale. All. Over. The. Shop. Chaotic. Frazzled. Scatterbrained. Discombobulated. There is no understanding of priorities. Work that needs to be done imminently can suddenly be put on the backburner and the work with no defined deadline gets started today. You totally forget appointments, places you need to be, things you've committed to. So, you quadruple check everything you have coming up but you overlook the thing you have now. You're late and scrambling. You rush out the door, check your pockets ten times to make sure you have the essentials, you get to the spot you left the car only to find it's not there.

Here we go. Alright, Xav, it's one of those days. All good. Structure. You need structure. Check your diary. Why do I have seven diaries? I should put these diaries in order. Let's start with that. The brown one is for ideas. The black one is for… This one's the day to day. Sweet. What day is it? Tuesday. No Wednesday! No, it's Tuesday. Should it be this difficult to - you had a wedding on Saturday you missed. Well, that's not good. Doctor's appointment today at nine – nope missed that. Hang on I thought they were calling me? No, I booked face to face. Right. This is a mess. This is carnage. Get it together. Diaries. I feel like I should be somewhere…What's the blue diary? Hang on why did I put them all on the floor? Which was the day to day one again? Shit. That Zoom started five minutes ago. If this requires a password I'm…Better cancel.

You're on the most meticulous factory floor. You've been tasked with overseeing the operation. It smells of disinfectant, the fluorescent lights are blinding and the machinery is so clean you can see your reflection in the metal. You're sure there should be people here but there aren't. A forging machine is producing nuts and bolts at a rapid rate. It's almost eery how seamless the person-less production line is. Out of your periphery you spy a vending machine with a solitary can of soft drink. You cannot imagine a world in which you don't have that soft drink. You take a step towards it. As you do an explosion echoes out across the factory. The machine has combusted. Nuts and bolts are flying into the air. You rush to find an emergency button. The ground is flooded with busted nuts and bolts. You start picking up scraps. The soft drink. You run towards the vending machine. The forging machine starts to whistle from the pressure. The emergency button. The floor is littered with nuts and bolts, you can't handle this mess. Pick them up! The whistling. Emergency button. Soft drink. The nuts and bolts continue to pile up as the whistling only gets louder.

The Elephant In The Room...

Suicide

I WAS TORN AS how to approach this. Writing in greater detail about this part of the bipolar experience, giving it a thought pattern and an image, I think would be irresponsible. This book is about resilience and a chance to give people an understanding of what bipolar is like. This is about living even when it's difficult.

In saying that there have been many times in my life where I have had to deal with thoughts of suicide. I have to face that here. I've lost people I care about to suicide. It shreds your heart to pieces. All you feel is sorrow so ubiquitous it follows you everywhere. We don't want to accept that thoughts of ending your life are present much less announce them to people. That's exactly why I needed to include this. We have to talk when it comes to this point. We have to let others help us in these times.

Now, why it gets to that point. When your thoughts are so damaging, relentless, hurtful, chaotic, brutal, you question whether it will ever end. After constantly feeling at war with your brain for an extended period of time you are simply out of answers. It's not the feeling of giving up it's the last desperate search for an answer.

After surviving the darkest times, you start to see all that is good in your life. When perspective finally arrives, you will feel a sense of gratitude that far outweighs the pain once felt. It may seem like it will never come but it does. There is always a chance to solve the issues that plague you. Fight with everything you have to not allow it to get to a place where suicide feels like the answer. If you find yourself there then I implore you to speak up and always continue to search for the antidote. There is going to be a way out of it. I write this from personal experience. The battle may be long but the tide will turn. Your fight and bravery will be rewarded with a new lease on life. Be strong.

A New Life

THE LIFE YOU knew for twenty-eight years feels like it was lived in the skin of another person. You can barely recognise that version of you. For the rest of your days, you can be the person you aim to be. All the pain, all that baffled and hurt you, made you feel like you were in a speeding car without a steering wheel, it's beginning to make sense. There's no more wondering why things feel so out of control. You know why. Now there can be progress.

Each day for years on end you have been toiling away in an open field building a humble shelter. You stack brick after brick from sunrise to sunset. Daily, you leave with calloused hands, tightened muscles and heavy eyes. Some days you're burnt and dehydrated, other days you're freezing cold and shivering. Brick after brick. You build and build. Though when you arrive each day the whole structure has collapsed and you have to start again. Until one day you arrive and the structure you've built has remained overnight. It's not perfect. There are gaps, cracks and holes but it's big enough to protect you, for the most part, from the sun and the rain. Despite its flaws, you built it and you can't help but feel a little pride.

With time I have learnt what I can do to keep myself as stable as possible. Emotions coming from a stable foundation are much easier to manage. My coping mechanisms are, of course, anecdotal and are what work for me. These things may resonate with you, they may not, they may serve as a leaping off point. Or maybe you just have to find your own. Finding your coping strategies is vital in aiming for stability. Waiting for problems to be fixed and solutions to magically appear will drive you mad because, well, they won't. The good news, it can get better.

Diagnosis

Heading into what the new world of properly acknowledging the obese elephant in the room was frightening. Diagnosing what it really was felt even more scary. Despite wanting the answer, I didn't know what it meant on the other side. When I heard the doctor say 'This is bipolar disorder', there was an immediate sense of relief even though I didn't fully know what I was in for going forward. I knew a little about it but I couldn't tell you about it in any depth. Then after two more GP's, a psychiatrist and a psychologist reaffirming the diagnosis including one saying 'This is the most obvious case I've bipolar I've ever seen.', the diagnosis was official.

Strangely the diagnosis gave me a sense of freedom. I know how that sounds, freedom from getting diagnosed with a chronic disease? It's an answer. You know what you're dealing with. There are ways to improve your life. It was the most significant moment in my life to that point. I'd had suspicions for about five years that bipolar disorder was what I had.

'We rarely diagnose under the age of 30. We like to treat the conditions before landing on bipolar. It's a disease not a condition so it's with you for life.' That's the other side…The reason you spent so many years avoiding this is you want to believe that what you have is something that will just go away of you'll overcome. For the rest of your days, you will be medicated, you will have to put in conscious work every day into your mental health and you will never be fully healed. This isn't about being cured it's about management. But they finally got it! Finally! And now what? Medication.

Medication

THE DIALOGUE AROUND medication can be difficult to stomach as someone who's life has changed for the better because of it. So many stories are about the journey to get off the meds. An example, Zach Braff's character in Garden State states the lithium he's on makes him feel 'numb' and he wants off it. His whole journey through the film is about getting off his medication and when he does so he has 'won'. Now he's fixed. It's a dangerous message. And it doesn't help when famous girthy little podcasters who have been kicked in the head too many times preach no vaccines to the masses and social media gets flooded with anti-medicine sentiment by Monster drinking flat earthers. The right medication saves lives. Simply put I wouldn't be here today without it.

I had my first appointment with a psychiatrist to get my medication sorted in the first COVID lockdown of 2020. 'It's going to be a bit of trial and error to get the right mix of medications and dosages. We're going to start you on one mood stabilizer and then reassess in a few weeks.' Right. A mood stabilizer. Makes sense. 'And an anti-psychotic to help you sleep.' Anti-psychotic? The joke I tried with the psychiatrist resulted in a slightly wry smile, if not a sympathetic one. 'Dude, I've got enough to deal with can't we call them pro-sanity's?' A weak joke but it was worth a shot. Clinicians find jokes about medicine about as funny as a recently divorced marriage celebrant officiating a wedding. Though he did put in my bipolar diagnosis report that I 'Used humour well'. Guess I'll take it. That was it. Concise, professional and expensive. 'There's a good website if you'd like to know more.' Really? A fucking website's going to be the thing that settles my bipolar? I hadn't considered the internet as a companion. Guess I could just create a mate out of AI.

'The other thing I should tell you is that while your body adjusts to the medication you will experience heightened anxiety and depression for three months.' Cause that seems fair being stuck inside a house with nothing to do, literally running the risk of being arrested if you stray too far from your house, already with heightened anxiety and depression. What they later told me was that it was actually six months 'We didn't want to overwhelm you at first by telling you six.'

When a month or two rolled around and my bipolar had not improved they started me on a second mood stabilizer and swapped out the anti-psychotic because it was making me groggy. As uncomfortable and frustrating as it was getting to the point where my medication was at the right level it was a necessary process. Stable was the goal. My emotions have a much more predictable pattern because of medication. Depressive and hypomanic periods now tend to last a few days to a week whereas before they would be much longer. The intensity of these periods is greatly lower now too. Prior to the medication I would experience emotions on the scale of catastrophic to stratospheric. Now it's more like melancholic to elevated. Life is manageable. I now take two mood stabilisers, lamotrigine and lithium, and an anti-psychotic, quetiapine, to sleep. All in all, that's nine pills per day. Morning, evening and night. Is it a lot of admin? Sure is. Was it worth it? Without a shadow of a doubt.

Speak Up & Ask For Help

When I was twenty-one, I ended up in hospital on suicide watch. I was pinned down in an ambulance and carted away. I woke up in the morning with a psychiatrist by my bedside. He told me that I needed to seek help. Believe it or not that wasn't the worst part. The worst part was I'd been at a fancy-dress party the night before and after it ended, I had my breakdown so I woke up dressed as Will Ferrell from 'Semi-Pro'. Hailing a taxi early in the morning in short shorts and a hospital band around my wrist was a pretty surreal experience. It's amazing that it took things to go to that extreme for me to do something. Yet…I didn't. I put it down to an isolated event and continued to push my issues and emotions down. To acknowledge this incident spoke to something larger was too confronting to deal with back then.

By the time I got diagnosed with bipolar I simply couldn't ignore it anymore. I filled in my family and friends and suddenly the burden of it all was lessened. I had networks available to me whenever I needed to get things off my chest. What I previously saw as a weakness, being honest about my vulnerabilities, became a strength. You are bolstered by sharing the load with people there who support you. What I also came to learn was how readily the people who love you are wanting to talk to you about things that are plaguing you. It's easy to forget that they want to help when you are scared of being helped.

When I was younger, I saw the problems I was having as part of life. Everyone experienced difficulties. Mine were maybe just a little more intense. You only know what you know. I would rationalise the irrational. The minute I handed myself over to professionals was when my life changed for the better. It only really dawns on you once you start moving forward. Being proactive to help yourself creates real pride.

Our minds can play the cruellest of tricks to prevent us from being happy. By speaking up, admitting you're in pain and need assistance and subsequently getting the help you need is giving yourself the permission to be happy.

Therapy

THERE IS NO question I'll do this for the rest of my life. My emotions feel most level when in regular therapy. There's one caveat to therapy. You have to want to go. When you're willing to open up and receive advice then you'll get what you need out of it. If you go in holding your cards to your chest like what I did earlier in my life then you'll be throwing money against the wall. It's also worth mentioning that this process might take time. I'm lucky to have found a psychologist that I click with however I had to go through a few that I didn't.

After starting therapy I've been amazed at how much baggage I've carried with me subconsciously through life. You'd be surprised how easily you will find something to work through in every session. On the times where I've gone into a session thinking I have nothing on my mind are often the ones that dig up issues I may have repressed.

When you land on the right person you almost develop a shorthand as they understand your history and you understand their vernacular. In working with a psychologist, I've been able to discover the root causes of ways my brain turns on itself. The word I'm familiar with is programming. My thought patterns had been set by things I had learned early on in life that stayed with me. I still feel as though I'm unplugging those wires and it is a concerted effort to do so.

By working with a psychologist or therapist you're given tools to aid you when previously you would be left to flounder or just ride it out. These tools can help disengage from damaging thought patterns and learn to navigate our way through emotions we find difficult. I would strongly recommend therapy to anyone and everyone. It's an investment in yourself and your future and worth every cent.

Booze & Drugs Aren't The Answer

SO MUCH OF what's important in managing bipolar is about controlling what you can control. When you turn to these vices your grip on control loosens. It's a seductive idea to mask your troubles rather than face them. Escapism is alluring but it's only a band aid. Cosmetic cuts can be healed by covering the surface. If the cut runs deeper then band aids will just fall away and the wound will become infected.

If you're manic you're more likely to overindulge or do and say regretful things. It's very easy to get carried away and very easy to make an idiot of yourself. When you're depressive there's a strong chance you'll end up miserable and teary. You don't want to be the person in the pub who the bouncer has to ask if 'Everything's okay' to. Been there. Not fun. If you do decide to get on it when you're out of sorts then there's the next day to consider too. Hangovers heighten the emotions felt beforehand and elongate them.

Now, I rarely drink. I know it doesn't always agree with me. I choose the occasions to drink carefully. If there's the slightest bit of sadness or worry or I'm in an elevated state I won't exacerbate that by drinking. It takes a lot more energy to get your way back to stable when you're masking it with depressants or stimulants.

Let Go Of The Past & Forgive Yourself

'Grant me the serenity to accept the things I cannot change, the courage to change the things I can, and the wisdom to know the difference.' The AA mantra is well known for a reason. What's done is done. We have to accept that. Holding on to what could or should have been does you no good in the now. Forgiving yourself will empower you to be better moving forward. You'll lose the present if you linger in the past. We will continue to make mistakes in the future. When we do spend energy in learning and loving.

Why is it that we feel the need to make ourselves feel so awful about our mistakes over and over? Why can I forgive terrible things done to me but find it so hard to find that forgiveness for myself for mistakes that pale in comparison? Your brain is crueller to you than any words you'd accept from people in your life. Berating yourself will only take you to darkness. If I spend too long ruminating on my regrets or mistakes, I end up going down a path of deep anxiety or depression. We have to focus on the fact that whatever we regret is a chance for us to learn.

Forgiving myself is a practice I struggle with yet always try as hard as I can. When you're able to send love to the person you see hurting in your past rather than needlessly chastising them you can start to heal. Even when you feel like what you have done wasn't good enough, you were acting with all the information and self-awareness you had at your disposal at that time. Make peace. Intellectually this is simple. Emotionally it's another story. Exhale it away.

Learn To Love Yourself

As much as we think some people are complete fuckwits there is a modicum of goodness in everyone. We can disagree, we can appose, even chastise but redeeming qualities will appear if you search hard enough. That pretentious person may be generous, the selfish person loving, the foul-mouthed bastard with a Southern Cross tattoo at the bar ordering Jager bombs after begging the DJ to play Pitbull…Loves his dog? We might have to dig but the good is there somewhere.

So, then it must be for you too. The term 'loving yourself' initially, and still kind of does, made me cringe. It sounded like a new-agey term to excuse being self-absorbed but it isn't. It's finding what is positive about you and embracing that. It's about self-respect and knowing your worth. To turn your perspective around and see yourself in this way can be bumpy initially. Particularly when it's not one you're used to.

When you're not in a position to love yourself, it can permeate into other elements of your life and behaviours like being unable to accept love from others. Alternatively, you can end up trying to fill the void by getting love from someone else but it papers over the cracks and is unsustainable.

One my twenty-ninth birthday, my first with diagnosed bipolar, my friends and family went to an enormous amount of effort in making it a wonderful occasion. At that point in my life, I was viewing myself in an entirely negative way and the attention, care and love was too much for me. It felt like I didn't deserve it and I didn't know how to process it. By the time my thirtieth came along I'd worked really hard to value myself and learnt to accept the love, care and effort that the people around me put into making it a special time in my life. A year before I was overwhelmed, the next year I had learnt to appreciate myself and enjoy the celebrations.

Philosophy

It's easy to dismiss philosophy as something a bloke wearing non-prescription reading glasses, carrying a leather satchel and wearing a mohair scarf at the theatre goes on about in a bid to sound interesting but there's value in exploring it.

We have yearned to understand the mind itself going back thousands of years. Enormous amounts of time and energy have been spent attempting to unlock the keys to happiness. So, why wouldn't we look for guidance from the people whose ideas have stood the test of time? If your writings on philosophy are still making an impact two thousand years later then there might just be something to them.

The Stoic's have been useful for me. They're ruthlessly pragmatic which is beneficial for someone whose emotions can get the better of them.

I've found philosophy teaches how thoughts and ways of thinking link to our emotions. From there you can work through them. It's helping us answer the how and why. Educating yourself on the machinations of your brain can help you to understand your pain and joy. Finding the ideas that align with you will help and you'll be the better for it. Do avoid the bloke with the leather satchel though. You'll never want to look into philosophy if you don't.

Art

As a society we have become overstimulated. From the moment we wake up we are checking social media, messages, emails, the news, stimulus on stimulus. It can be hard to find moments where we let our brain stop. So, when you're standing in front of a piece of art and forcing yourself to be still and absorb it, there's a peaceful quality to it.

Viewing artwork engages a different side of our brain. We're used to being given the whole story in visual form in the modern age through film and TV. With art we have much more creative license to find our own story in the work. There are a million different interpretations that can be had out of the one artwork. You may look at a painting one day and be entirely connected to it and the next another one grabs your attention.

There's also a freedom involved in looking at art. I can't help but dream up the context and creation of it, picturing that artist sitting down and concentrating, solving problems and finding satisfaction. Artists who lived their lives as destitute then have their work hanging in a gallery on the other side of the world hundreds of years later is remarkable in itself. It just so happens that one of those is Vincent Van Gough who is believed to have had bipolar and whose birthday is World Bipolar Day.

Art is one of our earliest forms of expression. It's a form of storytelling and that's what makes us human. So being around the work, the beauty, the history and the calmness of the environment is a soothing place for my brain. All the reasons listed above are why I've also found comfort in classical music. A classical composition provides more of an opportunity to create your story and can change from listen to listen. Like art, it's soothing and peaceful.

Writing & Creativity

As children we are all creative. We paint, draw, make music and write stories. I believe that we all have a creative streak inside of us and it's just like a muscle. If it's not exercised it goes away but it can be strengthened even if it has lay dormant.

My creativity started early and blossomed as I got older. The problem was that I had so much in my head that I didn't know where to put it. After such a long period of seemingly insurmountable and ubiquitous pain I decided to write. In some ways it was a hit and hope. After I was released from hospital on suicide watch I had to try something. I loved theatre so I wrote a play. It was semi-autobiographical, write what you know.

Suddenly I was able to explore and dissect all the issues that I was having and turn it into story. I've since learned that I see the world in stories. Ideas, concepts, they turn into narrative. People, their history, they turn into characters. All the creativity that was just festering in my head was able to be released. Instead of my own flaws I could focus on the flaws of a character for a while.

Writing looks different from person to person. It can be stream of consciousness, poetry, prose, word vomit, whatever works for you. The process writing down your challenges onto a piece of paper, out of your head, will be cathartic. Writing was really the first step for me to admitting something was wrong. It has dragged me through the toughest of times. So, try it. And don't judge what it is. Let it be your freeing expression and, hopefully, cathartic.

There are obviously other creative outlets outside of writing. For a while I painted terribly. I tried drawing and that was toddler level shit. Although I did enjoy the process of them both and will go back to it.

There are all sorts of ways you can express yourself creatively. You can sculpt, flower arrange, candle make, do a live drawing class of an old man with descending testicles, whatever you choose I genuinely believe in the positivity that creative endeavours can bring to someone. They're beneficial because there's a tangible element to them too. They require focus which means you aren't stuck in your head.

Nature

THE MAJESTY OF nature puts everything in perspective. The world exists without us, we need it, it doesn't need us. Yet how often do we take time to really appreciate it? As someone who lives in the city I can say not as much as I should. Watching the trees sway in the wind, feeling the grass between your fingers, looking at the waves caressing the sand, jumping in the ocean and feeling the salt water melt away anxious energy, staring at the sky and watching as the clouds slowly pass by calms the body and mind. It brings attention to the immediate.

In these moments I like to take time to think how many people around the world are being part of nature like I am. Picnics on the grass, jumping under waves, searching for patterns in the stars. For me it brings a sense of togetherness. When we aren't appreciating ourselves being in nature serves as a way of reigniting our appreciation for something.

To ease anxiety there's a simple way of calming yourself that works wonderfully in nature. All you do is focus on your senses. Ask yourself what can you see, touch, hear, smell and taste. Quickly you'll be able to centre yourself and be in the present.

Being in nature aligns us with the bigger picture, where we cannot be alone. Nature can be our companion when feel like we don't have one.

Explore

ADVENTURING IS ONE of life's great joys. The excitement of travelling to a city you've never been to before is experiencing everything for the first time. Stoic philosopher Seneca said that "We should take wandering outdoor walks, so that the mind might be nourished and refreshed by the open air and deep breathing." I love this quote mostly for the word wandering. We don't have to have a destination to get something out of going for a walk.

When I'm in a stuck in an emotional loop I will go back to parts of the city that I like but don't often get a chance to visit just to look around. In my own area I like to walk down streets around my house that I haven't been down before and treat it like I'm a tourist exploring the city. Or I will try and notice things I haven't before. Houses, shopfronts, signposts or even trees are new stimulus to engage my brain. It can be simpler. Stay with me here, even just trying a new food or beverage. It might sound trivial but experiencing something new, even on such a small scale, can be a little break from the monotony and repetitive nature of life. My aim in doing these simple things is to physically and mentally cut the power to an emotional loop and entice my brain to search outside of me.

Exercise

EXERCISE IS ESSENTIAL. That should be the end of it really. It's essential for your health, obviously, but it's crucial for your mental health too. In stable, depressive or hypomanic periods one thing that needs to stay consistent is daily exercise. I always start my day with it. Whether it's an intense weightlifting session, sprints, the spin bike or walking the dogs exercise will be a high priority. My mind labours when my body does. Exercising gets the day off to a positive start.

In depressive periods exercising feels like the worst possible way to spend your time. You'd rather have dinner with Scott Morrison. You're out of energy before you even start. Once you do every fibre in your body is asking for you to stop. These are the days where exercise is the most important. Depressive periods make exercise brutal but it's here where you see the greatest contrast and upside in regards to your mood.

When you're hypomanic exercise will feel great and you'll be able to push yourself like crazy but it can go too far. It's very easy to overexert and injure yourself when you have an untapped well of energy at your disposal. I have. If you injure yourself and can't exercise it's far worse than stopping a little earlier than you want. When you're robbed of the endorphin rush from exercise you feel how drastically it affects your mood.

My mood is always improved post exercise. Exercise means different things to different people. Whether it's high or low intensity it's worth doing. Make it a priority.

Moderate

THERE'S A WORLD in which you can say no to going to things and not feel like you're missing out. I wish I could tell that to myself in my early twenties. I socialised to the point I had no time to myself. To me if I missed out, I ran the risk of being abandoned as a friend. Amazing the thoughts that link back to your childhood. Abandoned by your father so you'll be abandoned by your friends. Just so you know they won't abandon you if you don't go to the pub on a Tuesday night for a cheap schnitzel.

Some of the over socialising was probably just to avoid having to face that I wasn't happy by myself but as I've come to know myself better, I've learnt that I'm an even split of introvert and extrovert. If you're an extrovert then you are energized by constant time spent with other people but if you're an introvert then taking time away to recharge is essential. Extroverts should still take time for themselves and introverts should still interact with others. As I'm right down the middle I need time to myself as much as I need time with my friends and family.

If you listen to your internal rhythm your body and brain will tell you when you are too distant or you need a break. When I have overcommitted socially, I have burned out and it has heightened my emotional state. Conversely, when I have undercommitted, I have found myself feeling lonely and isolated. Find your balance.

Practice Gratitude

STRESS AND IRRITATION hits like a truck at all sorts of random times. You're stuck on a bus next to a sweaty bloke who reeks of KFC, Optus has another nationwide service outage, Jordan Peterson releases another book, the Murdoch family will keep pumping bullshit into people's head for decades to come, you realise that in forty years the only sport you'll be playing is lawn bowls, you've been getting life advice from someone without a clue, you realise you're addicted to 'Married At First Sight' and houses don't cost thirty grand anymore. When our mental health is faltering these stresses only intensify and a positive outlook can easily become swallowed by a negative.

When I was in a long depressive period my psychologist suggested I write down a list of things I was grateful for. I started at the obvious destination, friends and family. It didn't take long to find more, my favourite places I've travelled to, my achievements, how we can fly around the world, the ocean, sport, films, music, books, my medication. I went down to the simplest pleasures, chocolate, every time someone spells my name wrong on a coffee order, a twenty-three degree day. Before I knew it, I'd written down one hundred things I was grateful for. A gratitude list is a powerful tool to get you to see the things that make you happy. It's simple and effective. From there you can take one of those things and implement it in your day and maybe turn it around.

We need to remind ourselves of all that is good in our lives and of the things we are lucky to have without comparison. If we get caught comparing then we aren't invested in being grateful. If we focus on ourselves, on our lives, on what is valuable to us then we can shift our brain from pessimism to optimism.

Stay True To Yourself

Over time you discover what your values, beliefs and morals are. These are the core principles in which you should stay true to. Of course, it's worth mentioning that to find what your standards and beliefs are, to grow, comes from introspection. Learn to be happy with what you offer and come to terms with the fact that not everyone will like you. That's okay. You won't like everyone either. You don't need to shapeshift in order to please anyone.

This shouldn't be conflated with stubbornness. The old 'This is who I am, take it or leave it' is fine if you can admit when you're wrong, acknowledge your shortcomings and apologise. When it's problematic is if you continue to hurt other people around you with no consideration of their feelings and are unmoved by that. Then you're just a dick. My aim is to constantly evolve and strive to be a better version of myself whilst keeping the DNA of who I am.

Be unapologetically you. Be authentic. Stand up for what you believe in. But don't be a dick.

Value Your Friends & Family & Choose Them Wisely

I'D BE NOWHERE without my friends and chosen family. Cherish the people you let into your inner sanctum. You want people in your life who can have the difficult conversations with you. You want people who will support and bolster you when you feel as though you can't do that yourself.

There's also a power in letting people go who no longer serve you. That may sound cynical but nostalgia is no reason to hold onto unconstructive relationships. Toxic people have a way of bringing out toxicity in you. It's like you can absorb it via osmosis. Just because someone says they love you doesn't mean they have your best interests at heart. Just because you share a last name doesn't mean you have to have them in your life if they continually make you feel like shit. If you can be critical in your thinking and truly ask yourself "Is this person bringing positivity into my life?", then you will find out who is worth your energy. Being prepared to make tough decisions and cut off pernicious people you will make you flourish on the other side of it.

Strong family connections and friendships are about support, loyalty, care, kindness and love. The family that remains a part of my life are incredible. For all the negativity I have received from some I can still confidently say I have a wonderful family. All my friends are emotionally intelligent and that is probably the greatest asset you can ask for. Healthy relationships mean you're listened to without judgement and offered words of kindness when needed. They are there for you when things are ugly, not just when you're up and about. It's more important to be present when tears flow than when there's laughter.

After I got diagnosed, I started telling the important people in my life that I love them often. You will never regret letting someone you care about know how you feel but you will regret it if they never hear it. I've found that opening up that channel has encouraged that dialogue to go both ways. Then, when times are tough, those words are spoken when you need them most.

Epilogue

All these tools, hobbies, distractions and past times are there to build foundations. They are an aid not a cure. My version of emotional normalcy looks very different to those without bipolar. The puzzle isn't solved, it can't be. I still have depressive periods, I still have hypomanic periods. The nature of the disease means that sometimes I'm struck with these periods out of nowhere and I feel as though I'm chasing my tail. That's when it's most difficult.

This book was a challenging undertaking. In writing Living With Bipolar it was painful, raw, upsetting but also cathartic. I was forced to face all the difficulties that are part of my life and therefore seeing how difficult it can be at times. There were moments I wasn't sure if I'd be able to finish it. To do that I had to remind myself as to why I started it in the first place.
I wanted to provide an authentic insight into bipolar. I wanted to help someone who was like me before I knew what this was. A lot of pain could've been avoided if I knew earlier.

If someone who is in the same position as I was reads Living With Bipolar and sees themselves in here, if it prompts anyone to get help or to a diagnosis, I will have succeeded in what I set out to do. If people who are struggling with the disease or any other mental health affliction can find solace in this then that's a win. If people who don't experience any challenges but want to know more learn something from this book then that's a win.

I used to feel like I was at war. Nowadays I feel like I have to put out spot fires. I've never been much of a planner and I suppose that comes from a history of not knowing where I'd be emotionally tomorrow or the day after. I was in a constant state of fight or flight. The future was just an out of reach concept that was either anxiety inducing or not designed for me to imagine. That's changed. Now I can see myself in ten years, twenty, fifty, I can look into the future and not be frightened. I see happiness, excitement and possibility.

What I yearned for but never grasped…Hope. Today, tomorrow, the future. The fact I fought through the trauma and had to struggle for years before getting the right diagnosis means I built resilience. Resilience runs through my blood. My brain won't defeat me.

Speak up. Reach out. Seek help. Forgive yourself. Love. Love others. Love yourself.

Criticizing yourself is easy. To love yourself is hard but worth the fight.

Acknowledgements

Special Thanks To

Mary Jane Coy, Pad Donohoe, James Donohoe, Jen Davidson, Cam Davidson, Geraldine Coy, Bryan Cockerill, Damian Willis, Michael Arvithis, Clark Wenborn, Lintyn Basha, Alex Still, James Daniel, Angus Moore, Mark Ilijas, Liam Carmody, Jordan Steer, Sam Masi, Jack Ballhausen, Timo Blundell, Nick Bradley, Emelia Griggs, Dave Woodland, Nick Denton, Lloyd Allison-Young, Jay James-Moody & Greg Moran.

Extra Special Thanks To

Matilda Coy, who was always there when things were most difficult and brings joy to all she encounters.

Bernice Lethlean, who is the most remarkable person I've ever met. Her warmth, support and love has brightened my life to a place I never thought it could be. I love you with all my heart.

About

Xavier Coy - Author

Xavier Coy is a Sydney based writer and actor. He started writing plays in 2014 and staged *Smokin' Joe*, *Caught Out*, *Distorted*, *Are You Listening Now?* and *Charles & Larry*. From there he went on to work in TV on Channel 10's *Five Bedrooms* whilst being part of development rooms along the way. In 2023 his short film *Fighting* premiered at the Sydney Film Festival.

"For me writing came out of necessity," Xavier says. "It began as a form of catharsis. I was struggling with my mental health and had to find a way to make sense of what was rattling around in my brain. As soon as I started, I never stopped. I was able to turn concerns, worries, fears and ideas into story. I found my release and consequently my vocation".

Michael Arvithis - Illustrator

Michael Arvithis is a Sydney-based fine artist and illustrator with a BFA in painting/drawing from COFA (present day Art & Design, UNSW). Michael has won numerous national art prizes and has illustrated both children's and adult books, as well as designing and illustrating marketing material for various independent theatre companies and music venues. Largely influenced by the Post-Impressionists, film history, 90s comic art and Francis Bacon, Michael's work ranges from dreamlike landscapes to comical satirisations of societal behaviour, to more surreal depictions of the darker parts of the human psyche. His works often explore loneliness, urban lifestyles, altered states of mind, human connection and his family's Greek roots. To contact Michael, visit his instagram page 'michaelarvithisartist' or email him at michaelarvithisart@gmail.com.

www.ingramcontent.com/pod-product-compliance
Lightning Source LLC
Chambersburg PA
CBHW041647160426
43202CB00004B/18